Capital Formation and Entrepreneurship in Indian Agriculture

About the Author

A. Ghosh, M.A., Ph.D., was Senior Professor in Economics, Jadavpur University till 1986. Previously, he has been in the staff of the Indian Statistical Institute working with Professor P.C. Mahalanobis; in the Department of Applied Economics, Cambridge University working with Professor Richard Stone; a Research Fellow in the London School of Economics with Professor D.V. Glass; and in the Harvard University Research Project working with Professor Wasilly Leontief. He has also served the United Nations as adviser in the ESCAP, UNIDO and ECA working on problems of development of the entire Afro-Asian region. In the course of his work, he has published a considerable number of papers and books on different aspects of the development of Asian countries in general and India in particular.

CAPITAL FORMATION AND ENTREPRENEURSHIP IN INDIAN AGRICULTURE

A. GHOSH

CONCEPT PUBLISHING COMPANY, NEW DELHI-110059

Cataloging in Publication Data—DK
Courtesy: D.K. Agencies (P) Ltd. <docinfo@dkagencies.com>

Ghosh, A., 1921-
Capital formation and entrepreneurship in Indian agriculture/ A. Ghosh.
p. ; cm.
Includes bibliographical references (p.)
Includes index.
ISBN 818069142X

1. Agriculture—Economic aspects—India. 2. Agricultural industries—India—Capital investments. 3. Entrepreneurship—India. I. Title.

DDC 338.109 54 21

ISBN 81-8069-142-X

First Published 2005

Published and Printed by
Ashok Kumar Mittal
Concept Publishing Company
A/15-16, Commercial Block, Mohan Garden
NEW DELHI-110059 (India)

Phones : 25351460, 25351794
Fax : +91-11-25357103
Email : publishing@conceptpub.com

Preface

The present report deals with the trend of Capital Expenditure and Capital Formation in Indian Agriculture. In the later part, it has also been our objective of noting the changes in the structure of Indian agriculture and its relation with capital consisting of both personal savings and bank loans. Further, we have also tried to trace flow of capital in building up the infrastructure of a very primitive agricultural economy which has been aptly described as a land-labour-bullock economy with land-bullock and labour as the major elements of capital formation which except labour has been very small in the early period. We have also tried to show that the planning process in this country came as an injection of a huge fund in agriculture which was reflected in gradual alteration of the investment climate of agriculture all over the country. There was, it seemed, a general awareness of the possibility of a breakthrough from the primitive form of agriculture which has been going on for a long time in this country. The cultivator took advantage of this changing capital structure and at least, in certain prosperous part of India this change was almost perceived as a revolution in agricultural technology specially in the Northern and Western part of the country. In the other parts where the change was not so significant it was seen that the basic poverty of very large section of the cultivators prevented them from absorbing this revolutionary change. We may sum up as follows. Capital investment of low income household remains predominantly traditional and the only change most cultivators tried was to secure more land. The moderate and the middle income household in agriculture took a greater interest in irrigation equipments and agricultural machinery and thus, ushered in a more modern type of agriculture by making a better use of the availability of more funds from the

Government and cooperatives and other institutional credit agencies. But for the very poor cultivators with so low a size in holding household assets that they could not avail of the institutional credit. The were forced to go to the private agencies of the old usurious type and in general, their situation remained at this point at a very low level equilibrium. It is generally felt that for bringing about a significant change in the technology of primitive agriculture, it is necessary to utilise the poorest level of cultivators who has always been running into a vicious circle of poverty, pressure of population and lack of even reasonable resource to maintain their existing standard: it is very difficult to do anything significant in this class without syphoning off the very large surplus labour and the ever increasing population pressure in order to shift this depressed group away from agriculture to small scale urban industries so that, there may be a general structural shift in the technology and a major change of moving from very small scale poverty ridden primitive agriculture of a subsistence type.

The completion of the project work has been made possible by the active involvement of project team located in the Calcutta Project Office. In this respect, I mention the name of Shri Sudhir Bhattacharyya, formerly of the National Sample Survey Organisation who prepared the original proposal of the project and later worked as an adviser to the team members from the beginning till the completion of the report. I must mention the name of Shri Ajoy Kr. Guha, formerly of Indian Statistical Institute and Calcutta Port Trust who was attached to the project as a Senior Research associate and who prepared the schedules and the instructions for the investigators, organised the survey work at several specified villages of one district of West Bengal and finally prepared the report in collaboration with Shri Sudhir Bhattacharyya.

A. GHOSH

Contents

List of Tables

1

Introduction

Despite the concerted efforts of the government through planned development programme implementation over the last three decades and half, there has been little sectional transformation of Indian economy and agriculture still remains one of the most important sectors in the national economy. According to the 1981 census, agriculture remained the means of livelihood of about 70 per cent of the total population of the country and together with its allied sectors, it contributed about 37 per cent of the national income calculated for 1985-86. In view of such overwhelming dominance of agriculture in national economy, the key to the significant structural transformation of Indian economy obviously, lies in bringing about a rapid change of the existing capital structure of Indian agriculture for transforming it from a predominantly subsistence sector to a surplus generating business and industrial sector.

India undoubtedly has passed over the stage when Indian agriculture was labelled as a simple land-labour activity, a pre-capitalist sector with very little formation of reproducible tangible capital. But at best, till the country entered into the era of development planning after independence, Indian agriculture could be described as a land-labour-bullock economy. According to an available estimate,[1] investment in agriculture on implements, bullocks, irrigation and land on the eve of First Five Year Plan was of the order of Rs. 2300crores, 73.7 per cent of which was spent on bullocks alone and for other items, such as, irrigation, tools and implements, improvement of land 14.1 per cent, 7.1 per cent and only 4.1 per cent were spent respectively. Very little was usually spent till then on fertiliser and major portion of whatever little was spent on fertiliser, was only for plantation.

Till that time, one might say, agriculture in India followed the traditional path in so far as capital expenditure and capital formation was concerned and depended largely on human and animal labour and on natural endowment of seasonal rain-water required for cultivation. The use of tools, machinery and other agricultural implements were at the irreducible minimum and the resources spent on irrigation was only marginal and the beneficiaries were only a small section of rich farmers.

The end of Second World War, the partition of the country and its aftermath — the influx of millions of uprooted refugees in the country across the border and consequential severe shortage of food created an unprecedented situation which forced the government to make concerted effort for raising the agricultural production to a higher level within the shortest possible time-span by taking recourse to development programme through planned investment in agriculture. The Central Government had to assume the role of entrepreneurs in the agricultural sector which needed a big push with a view to bring about a complete overhauling of the on-going traditional technique of production for quickly achieving the objective of the increase of production, as also, productivity. Agriculture in India, the most critical area in the country's economy, needed that big push to meet this challenge posed before the country.

The impact of this direct intervention through massive planned investment and also through pumping of finance, in the form of providing credit facilities from banks and other financial institutions to cultivator households was quite impressive. This new agricultural strategy adopted by the Central Government attempted to attack the problem from different directions. But the main thrust of the strategy was on changing the production technique through the creation of congenial condition for the application of new capital inputs, such as, chemical fertiliser, improved and high yielding varieties of seeds, pesticides etc., and most importantly, the building up and expansion of irrigation facilities to a wider extent. The massiveness of the state intervention can easily be judged from the figures of the amount of allocation of the total plan outlay for agriculture and irrigation available from official statistics. The percentage of outlay on agriculture and irrigation was highest in the first plan, viz. 31 per cent of the total plan outlay and was between 20 to 25 per cent in all other plans upto the Seventh Plan. As the total outlay in each plan was increased, the outlay of agriculture and irrigation was also increased in every plan. In addition to the plan outlay, through nationalisation of banks in 1969 and a very wide extension of co-operative banking facilities, availability of credit facilities to the cultivators at the time of their credit need, had been immensely increased.

Through the adoption and implementation of the new agriculture strategy, a real break through in Indian agriculture could be achieved both from the point of view of expenditure on capital inputs and on formation of new tangible capital base, such as, irrigation potential, soil conservation etc., made during 1960-61 to 1986-87, the achievement had been noteworthy. The available official statistics on the progress of agriculture during 1960-61 to 1985-86 clearly substantiated the above contention and since 1960-61, a gradual but steady change from the land-bullock to seed-fertiliser-water technology in agriculture could be discerned. The big push for change applied by the central Government had also its impact on private investment on improved seeds, fertilisers, and also on farm assets like pumpsets, tubewells and also on tractors, modern agricultural implements and tools though not so extensively as on modern inputs and irrigation infrastructure.

The adoption of the new agricultural strategy has resulted in progressive expansion in area under crop, total production and also productivity. The results achieved, particularly for rice, wheat and other food crops were impressive. This new strategy has also expanded rural employment opportunities and helped curbing of rural idleness and under-utilisation of work capabilities of rural workforce by more job opportunities provided through changes introduced in cropping pattern and in shifting from mono-crop to multiple crop in cultivation. Also, it created more work for hired labour and thereby, increased their wage rate and income. The adoption of new strategy had also strengthened backward linkage between agriculture and industry by creating additional demand of industrial products, such as, fertilisers, pesticides, pumpsets, machinery and tools, power and power equipments used for irrigation required in agricultural farms which adopted the new technology.

But what has been stated above relates to the country as a whole and is certainly not valid for the different regions of a vast country like India. The new strategy has definitely benefited and improved the conditions of agriculture in those areas where conditions were favourable for the adoption of such strategy. Agriculture still remains dependent on vagaries of nature in quite a large tract of the country. Small farmers with less land, poor finance and poor credit worthiness have not been able to venture into the adequate utilisation of the new strategy in their farms. Quite likely the vast majority of poor peasants having owned or possessed only a small parcel of uneconomic holding have not been able to derive any substantial benefit of the new strategy.

This means that uneven development towards change in the capital structure, both variable capital in the form of modern capital inputs and the fixed tangible capital in private agricultural farms in the different regions of the country has led to slower growth rate of agricultural production and perpetuation of rural poverty and backwardness. The bold initiative taken by the government through the massive public investment made in Indian agriculture towards building-up a strong base of modern capital structure, such as, extensive irrigation potential improvement of land, drainage and flood control, etc., and provision of supply facilities to intending users the modern capital inputs, like, improved seeds, fertilisers, etc., had not produced anticipated results as the derived benefits could percolate down to only a small section of the cultivating community and that also remained restricted to some selected regions of the country.

In the context of the pattern of growth and the structure of capital formation in Indian agriculture broadly outlined above, importance of the study on the trend and nature of capital expenditure and capital formation need not be emphasised. The need for such study assumes more importance as the country has abundant supply of unutilised labour and a cultivating household will always try to make judicious combination of capital with labour to maximise the production and their gains and that will ultimately determine the structure of capital in their farms. The study is also important as it is linked-up not only with the growth of agriculture itself but also with the overall development and growth of Indian economy because the growth of manufacturing and other sector of the economy is linked up with the growth of agriculture.

This study aims at finding out the characteristics of the pattern of the capital expenditure and capital formation in Indian agriculture as a whole and also how that obtains differently in different states. Also an attempt will be made to identify the major obstacles and difficulties which impede the progress of the process of change and modernisation of capital structure in the different parts of the country and under various economic environment, congenial or otherwise, prevailing therein. A comparative study of the macro picture with a snapshot picture taken in a case study undertaken in West Bengal has also been attempted.

The study regarding the nature and characteristics of capital formation in Indian agriculture is beset with many difficulties. One of the difficulties to be confronted lies in the area of conceptualising capital formation. Broadly speaking, the capital is constituted of both the variable and the tangible fixed capital. While the farmer includes all kinds of investment providing factor inputs, namely, improved seeds, fertilisers, the latter stands for the additions to durable capital assets, such as, implements, tools, machinery, construction and major improvement in farm buildings, improvement on land, namely, soil conservation, bunding of land for irrigation. The expenditure made on both variable and fixed capital taken together is termed capital expenditure. Theoretically, investment made for improving the quality of human resources can be brought under capital investment also. Capital formation in agriculture also generally includes investments made on infrastructure and also on institutional changes brought into operation. But we shall dwell in this study on 'capital expenditure' and the 'fixed capital formation' in farm business as adopted in 'All India Debt and Investment Survey', conducted jointly by Reserve Bank of India and the National Sample Survey Organisation (NSSO). In this study our concern is only on private capital formation in Indian agriculture though it is a fact that the government, since the inception of planning process in the country, has made the major contribution in building up the massive irrigation potential, improvement of soil and also other relevant infrastructure for all-round development of agriculture in the country.

The other difficulty which restrict the scope of the study is the availability of the necessary data at a sufficiently disaggregated level. Of course, since the conduct of decennial survey jointly by the National Sample Survey Organisation and the Reserve Bank of India, the position regarding the availability of data has improved, but the data base do not provide all the different aspects of the nature of capital formation in Indian agriculture. The basic unit for data collection on the All India debt and investment surveys is the household and all the data on capital expenditure and capital formation, therefore, relates to the household as the economic unit. In our study, we have drawn heavily on the RBI survey data but have also used the data presented in several case studies on capital formation in Indian agriculture conducted by various researchers. We have also used relevant official statistics on different aspects of the agricultural situation in India, available in published form. Finally, as an integral part of this study, we have the data collected from the village survey conducted in 12 villages in the two districts of West Bengal, Bardhaman and South 24-Paraganas which provides a micro picture on the characteristics of capital formation in two different economic environments in the state of West Bengal which will be juxtaposed against the macro picture of the nature of capital formation in Indian agriculture with a view to drawing meaningful conclusion emanating from the study undertaken.

The present report, it must be remembered has a very modest scope which has been discussed. There are many points to note with regard to the limitation of this report; the first major limitation is that, while some previous studies have been reviewed by us with regard to capital formation, our own study is only confined to a direct study of several villages selected at random in two districts in West Bengal. Though comparison has been made with national sample survey and Census report, it has been pointed out that this direct comparison is open to grave doubts. The nature of the economy of two districts of Bengal cannot by any stretch of imagination be compared with the all India study. We can only say that where they agree with the all-Indian study say they may give us some satisfaction as they confirm our own study. But where they do not confirm it is difficult to say anything very definite.

The second most important point to note is that while we have made a study based on a snapshot of a very small portion of Bengal, the nature of capital formation is based on many historical and geographical factor which play their part in determining the course of capital formation. The changing nature of the economy of Indian also involves great social change and cultural transformation both in villages and cities along with technical changes. The present study considers mainly the technical and economic side in a narrow restricted way. Actually it is felt that a techno-economic study is quite different from a socio-economic study. A socio-economic study by definition is far more complicated and requires elaborate study in more depth. It is our plan, at a later stage to try to do a more broad based study which will also involve capital formation, the influence of social changes which interact with economic changes. The totality thus, of a grand picture involves much bigger canvas in space and time. It is our objective to make such a grand unified picture at a later period if the necessary resources are available. But so long as that is not available we should remember that the present study is an incomplete structure of steel and concrete without the binding cement and mortar, fixture and fittings, which together make the construction realistic and socially useful. The present study thus, is only a foundation of the first part and lot more has to be done to make it realistic and useful.

The arrangement of the Report is as follows: In chapter 2, a brief review of the contemporary literature on the subject is given. Chapter 3, deals with the analysis of the available secondary data on capital expenditure and capital formation in agriculture to give a macro-picture on the nature of capital expenditure and capital formation in Indian agriculture. Chapter 4 discusses the results of the case study undertaken as a part of the present study in two districts of West Bengal. In Chapter 5, the results of a probing inquiry carried out into the official records of the two lead banks operating in the corresponding police station areas where the case study has been undertaken with a view to ascertaining the nature of the credit deposit flow from and to the commercial banks has been presented. Concluding observations and recommendations are given in Chapter 6.

Note

1. Tara Shukla, *Capital Formation in Indian Agriculture*, Vora and Co., Bombay, 1965, p. 151.

2

A Brief Review of Contemporary Literature on Capital Formation in Indian Agriculture

In the context of development, the shortage or inadequate supply of capital resources, required for proper utilisation of country's productive potential and also for the expansion of productive capacity to meet the increasing domestic as well as export needs, have long been recognised as major factors that impede or slow down development and growth of economy in underdeveloped countries.

The intensive search by economists and researchers to identify the causes and to ascertain the consequence of capital shortage and also to find out ways and means to augment the existing stock of capital resources has been a continuing exercise. Literature on the subjects are, therefore, plenty. But although agriculture occupies a crucial position in the economy of many of the underdeveloped countries including India, their study on capital formation in agriculture has not been given adequate attention. The problems of conceptualisation, the applicability of the concepts in the condition of the concerned countries, non-availability of the necessary data with sufficient disaggregation over a large number of time intervals and lastly, the problem of valuation of the various items of capital employed in a largely unorganised and household based agriculture are probably the major hindrances that weaken the search on this topic. To the students of economics of underdevelopment, the writings of R. Nurske (1962)[1], S. Kuznets, T. Schultz (1960)[2], A. Lewis (1957)[3], and H. Singer (1962)[4], are well-known as they, besides presenting the theoretical framework for the study on the problems of capital formation, also throw light on the hazy concepts of capital in agriculture. These writings, apart from discussing various aspects of the problem of capital formation in agriculture, mainly suggested various different hypotheses to establish their respective stand points for identifying the crucial determinants which, according to their understanding, causes the shifts and the shape of the demand and supply schedules of new capital in agriculture.

The writings aparts, the most valuable contributions to the study of capital formation in Indian agriculture has been made by Tara Shukla (1965)[5]. Although, Indian agriculture has traversed a long path since 1965 and the situation of Indian agriculture, especially with regard to capital formation, has changed a lot, the basic formulations made in her study, still remains valid.

It was unfortunate that she could not handle and make use of the large amount of data which started forthcoming, since, the publication of results of all India debt and investment surveys conducted in 1961-62, 1971-72 and 1981-82; this flow of new data could have enabled her to make some more conclusive generalisations on many aspects of the subject of her inquiry.

Besides offering a discourse on the concept and measurement of capital which still remains a hazy area at least, in so far as the application of the concept to the condition in Indian agriculture is concerned, she has extensively dwelt on the theoretical framework for the study of capital formation in general and that for Indian agriculture in particular. In the latter she has included topics, such as, capital rationing, role of credit agencies and most importantly the impact of family-farm combination on capital formation. This analysis will help the researchers to delve deeper into the problems of capital formation in Indian agriculture making use of the required data becoming available now in the country.

The other problem which still disturbs researchers is the problem of netting. The issues like consumption of capital and loss of capital still remain the headache of data collection agencies. Though, some attempt has been made in the recent surveys to collect data on these two items, one is not sure about the reliability of the data due to the incompetence of the different informants, many of whom are not aware of the difference between gross and net value and its implication for data on capital formation. In Tara Shukla's study, however, this problem has been adequately dealt with to derive the net from the gross value making use of the data obtained from different sources.

The last important topic that has been ably handled in her study is the trend in stock of capital in agriculture in different states. The varying geographical climatic and economic conditions obtaining in different regions and states of the country contribute in various ways to the growth of agriculture and also the growth of the stock of capital in agriculture there. She has discussed the problem at length and has built up a time series for different capital items separately and for a selective combination of some of those items for a selective combination of some of those items to point out how, depending on the typical condition prevailing in a state, the choice of capital items differs and some items get priority over others in some states though the same priority is not given to the same item in other states.

P.G.K. Panikar's study (1967)[6] on capital formation in Indian agriculture may be considered an attempt to establish as untenable the view points offered by Nurske, Lewis and Singer under the conditions prevailing in Indian agriculture. The alternative hypothesis offered by Panikar is that low investment in traditional agriculture is due to backward technology. The conclusions formulated in his paper are given below:

The rate of capital formation in Indian agriculture is low. Superficial observation would attribute this to low savings, absence of integration between saving and investment, lack of entrepreneurship, etc., but on a closer scrutiny these appear to be only proximate causes, if not mere statistical association.

The hypothesis offered here is that capital formation is a function of the level of technology. Under the circumstances, the return to investment in such agriculture are apt to be low, and therefore, the incentive to invest weak. Investment rate will pick up with the appearance on the rural landscape of new inputs which embody modern technology. The hypothesis seems to stand the test of reason as well as empirical verification.

But while suggesting his alternative hypothesis, Panikar seems to have attached less importance to two institutional factors which motivate the growth of Indian agriculture, perhaps more significantly, than the factor embodied by new technology. The two factors are: (i) the size of farm-land the cultivator either own or possess; and (ii) the availability of easy credit facility the lack of which fails to provide the required fund the cultivators urgently require for introduction of new technology in his farm business.

It is generally acknowledged that the number of cultivator households with farm-land of size less than 2 acres is enormously large and also they are not considered very much credit-worthy even by public credit institution. In this context, in many cases the question of economic viability in preferring new technology to the traditional one in such small farms having also surplus household labour at their disposal remain uppermost in their mind in taking decision either in favour or against the introduction of new technology. Thus, the decision making with regard to introduction of new technology, most probably, depends more on other factors, such as, size-distribution pattern of farm-land, the extent of credit availability and the stock of surplus household labour. Panikar's hypothesis, thus, may work very well for relatively prosperous cultivator households, having medium or large size farm-land, of whom the 'appearance on the rural landscape of new inputs which embody modern technology' may help picking up investment rate in agriculture, the investment being oriented towards using modern inputs and also transforming the capital structure of their farm business. But, unfortunately such cultivator households in most parts of rural India constitute a small proportion of the total number of cultivator households at least in the major part of East and South India.

The importance of 'other factors' rather than the 'level of

technology' has been highlighted in a paper of Dr. B. Misra and S.C. Mallick (1969)[7]. Their conclusions are based on three studies conducted in Chittoor Taluka, Andhra Pradesh in 1965, in Cuttack district, Orissa in 1966 and in Guntur district, Andhra Pradesh in 1967. All the three studies had the same objectives, i.e., of examining the effect of irrigation, urbanised ways of living and size of holdings on capital formation.

The three important findings of the study are: (i) level of irrigation, the extent of urbanisation and size of land-holdings have positive effect on capital formation; (ii) higher the household income, the greater is the percentage of income devoted to capital formation; (iii) regional differences emerging out of different geographical, climatic and social variation of population do not contradict the above hypothesis.

The authors, however, have not explained why they considered 'income' as an independent factor. Is it not a fact that the factors 'income' and 'size of land holding' are positively correlated and it is the size of land holding which determine the scale of farm business and thereby the level of household income in the rural household. Of course, the enhancement of household income caused by urbanised and other income earning practice household non-farm business may not always be dependent on the size of farmland and consequently the scale of farm business.

Our observation on Panikar's paper made earlier in this chapter has partially been corroborated by the findings of another paper entitled 'Investment behaviour of traditional and modern farm'—A competitive study by M.G. Ghosh[8].

In this paper, instead of categorising farms into 'prosperous' and 'backward' made by us for the case study, the author has categorised the farms into 'modern' and 'traditional'. He designated the farms as 'modern' in the sense that they have partly adopted modern practices, are fully aware of its potentialities and are on the threshold of accepting it as a feasible business proposition and the traditional farms have been defined as farms which are generally owner operated and are following the traditional methods of cultivation. His study is based on two village surveys conducted in two sets of selected village ('modern' and 'traditional') in the district of Birbhum, West Bengal. The important observations of the author are:

1. There exists little difference in the intensity of cropping and the average yield rate of crops between the different size-group of farms in the traditional sector. But in the modern farms, there is wide difference in the intensity of cropping as well as the average yield of crops between the large size farms on the one hand and small and medium farms on the other.
2. Although, as compared to the traditional farm, expenditure on new technological inputs both per acre and per farm in the 'modern' group indicates a complete departure from the past practices, the new technology that has been adopted by the farmers is generally not labour-saving.
3. The traditional farmers still consider land as the most important of all assets for augmenting their income. But the 'modern' group seems to have acquired the knowledge that income can be raised by increasing the economic supply of land as opposed to its physical supply through the use of new technology.
4. The pattern of investment followed by the traditional farms is just to maintain the existing level of production and the only way to stimulate the growth in such farms lies in raising the level of efficiency of the factor inputs which involve substantial amount of expenditure for the development of infrastructure. Such investment creates the congenial condition and farmers also become aware of the potentialities of supplementary investments, but the lack of availability of either internal or external fund may act as barrier for them to escape the 'low level equilibrium trap'. In the case of modern farms, evidences nevertheless indicate that the development and introduction of the new technology accompanied with investment by government tend to induce capital expenditure by farmers.

5. Availability of credit in adequate quantity of appropriate interest rate has also a bearing on the extent of capital investment by farmers.

Ghosh, however, has not given a clear view as to which of the three factors—modern technology, or the rate of interest, or the size of farm holding, plays the key role in stimulating investment to add to the existing stock of capital. Maybe, by way of categorising of farms into 'traditional' and 'modern' he wants by implication, to assign the principal role to the size of landholding of farms as his 'modern' farms are constituted of only 'medium' and 'large' farms. But the real farm management operation may not be that simple and having considered that he has also recognised that 'appropriate interest rate' to obtain adequate quantity of credit has a bearing on the extent of capital investment to be made by farmers. We are inclined to conclude that not one but combination of few important factors, namely, the size of farm-land, the rate of interest and also perhaps the new technology acting in unison determine the demand as well as the supply of capital in Indian agriculture.

We shall conclude our discussion in this chapter by taking note of an interesting paper of Ashoka Rudra and *et al.* (1969) entitled "Big Farmers in Punjab"[9] based on a survey carried out in Punjab villages. They have defined 'Big farmers' as only the farmers having the size of land holding 20 acres and above and satisfying few other criteria and have categorised those farms as capitalist farms. They have estimated that, of the total number of farms in Punjab, such farms are only 3 per cent. Mentioning of this paper is considered relevant as it reveals to what extent, even in a state like Punjab, the most developed in the country in so far as development of agriculture is concerned, the size of land-holding of farms is crucial in deciding the nature and amount of capital investment, particularly on capital items like agricultural machinery, irrigation, equipments in farm business. The results of the study has shown that even in farms having land-holding size up to

30 acres, the size of capital expenditure on tractors, tubewells and pumpsets etc., remains moderate, the size of investment on such items starts ascending in farms having land-holding size 30 acres or more and it takes significantly large size only in farms having the size of holding 100 acres or more. The situation, most likely, will be similar in Haryana and also in the Western Uttar Pradesh and also in some of the areas of Maharashtra and Gujarat, particularly in the sugarcane and cotton growing areas.

But Rudra has added a new dimension to the study. His study reveals that the owners of very large sized holding whom Rudra has characterised as gentleman farmers pump-in large amount of funds in their agriculture-business. These farmers have roots also in industries and business in foreign countries where from the syphon-out funds and invest in agriculture in their home country for purchasing more land and for modernising the capital structure in agriculture and thereby their farm-holding increases in size and the modern machinery and tools in their farms also grow faster in number.

One last point on the change of technology and this persistence of small farms which has been often ignored is the growing pressure of a fast rising population coupled with the laws of inheritance which lead to smaller and smaller farms to persists on the very verge of bankruptcy. It is a fact that agriculture has pertly been on a subsistence level as with subsequent generation the original farm land had to be distributed into smaller and smaller parcels which more families cannot afford to leave as alternate work in rural and urban area are growing very slowly.

Unfortunately, in India agriculture development has two often been divorced from the growth of population and laws of inheritance owing to the lack of a holistic approach to available land and capital and its size from generation to generation. It is in this respect the sharp change in population size by state regulation is a pointer for Indian political and economic pundits who study this problems as a separate field of study.

Notes

1. Ragnar Nurske: *Problem of Capital Formation in Underdeveloped Countries*, Basil Blackwell, 1962.
2. T.W. Schultz: *Transforming Traditional Agriculture*, Yale University Press New Haven, USA, 1964.
3. W. Arther Lewos: *The Theory of Economic Growth*, George Allen & Unwin, 1957.
4. Hans Singer, *International Development*, McGraw Hill Book Company, 1964.
5. Tara Shukla: *Capital Formation in Indian Agriculture*, Vora & Co. Pvt. Ltd., 1965.
6. P.G.K. Pannikar: Capital Formation in Indian Agriculture, Conference Number of the *Journal of the Agricultural Economics Association*, 1969.
7. B. Misra and S.C. Mallick: *Factors Influencing Capital Formation in Agriculture*, Conference Number of *Journal of the Agricultural Economics Association*, 1969.
8. M.G. Ghosh: *Investment Behaviour of traditional and modern farm*, Conference Number of the *Journal of the Agricultural Economics Association*, 1969.
9. Ashok Rudra *et al.*: Big Farmers of Punjab, *Economic and Political Weekly*, December 27, 1969.

3

Trends of Private Capital Expenditure and Capital Formation in Indian Agriculture

A Macro Profile

In so far as the technique of production is concerned, Indian agriculture followed the traditional path over many years in the past till the country entered into the planning era in 1950-51. The condition of agriculture, which remained predominantly a subsistence sector, was not favourable for individual private cultivator to venture on their own a big leap for a speedy development of agriculture. A big external push by some central authority for its escalation to a higher level of development was considered an urgent need. This initiative was taken through planned outlay on agriculture and irrigation by the government at the Centre. In this respect the Central Government functioned like a financial authority to apply that big push. Such intervention, besides building up extensive base of irrigation potential by implementing major, medium and minor irrigation projects and building up of required infrastructural facilities also helped in making available to the cultivator the new technological inputs, such as, improved seeds, chemical fertilisers etc., in the process this move created a new investment climate favourable for the cultivating communities to incur various kinds of capital expenditure, a part of which, of course, was spent in acquiring tangible fixed capital required for farm business.

Although, to start with, the recorded progress was slow but gradually it gained momentum and as time passed both the size and content of capital expenditure changed progressively. Given the different natural endowment relevant for cultivation, obtaining in different parts of the country, the change brought about by taking advantage of the altered investment behaviour of the cultivating community, was not uniform throughout the country. The pattern of capital investment obviously was influenced largely according to the ability as also the enterprise of the cultivating community which differed in different parts of the country. But despite the uneven condition prevailing in different parts of the country the overall impact of new types of capital investment on agriculture was fairly strong as the capital structure of Indian agriculture started taking a new pattern and agricultural production recorded a significant growth.

In this chapter, we shall discuss, the trend of dimensions of the change of capital expenditure and capital formation in farm business brought about in rural areas by the cultivator households in the country and in the major states. The relevant data used in the discussion relates to the farm business of the cultivator households carried out in the rural areas as the focus of the present study is on the nature of capital formation in agricultural economy mainly in rural India.

Most of the data presented here are based on the results of the all India debt and investment surveys conducted in joint collaboration of Reserve Bank of India (RBI) and the National Sample Survey Organisation (NSSO) in 1961-62, 1971-72, 1981-82. Since the RBI has not so far published the 1981-82 survey results, we have to depend on some aggregated results published in the NSSO Report (Report No. 334 mimeographed). Some of the statistical information relating to agriculture published in different official publication have also been used in the discussion whenever considered necessary.

Concept and Definition

Gross capital expenditure increases the productive capacity of the enterprise. Conceptually, the gross capital expenditure is constituted of : (i) the expenditure made to maintain the capital intact, i.e. the maintenance cost, and (ii) the expenditure incurred on major improvement, construction and purchase of new capital items which leads to the formation of fixed capital assets. The latter alone is taken into account to estimate the value of fixed capital formation while the two together constitutes gross capital expenditure in farm business. Gross capital expenditure incurred for the purpose of cultivation may be listed as follows:

(a) purchase of land,
(b) purchase of land right,
(c) reclamation of land,
(d) bunding and other land improvement,
(e) orchards and plantations,
(f) wells, tubewells,
(g) other irrigation resources,
(h) agricultural implements, machinery and transport equipments,
(i) farm house, farm and cattle sheds,
(j) purchase of livestock,
(k) other capital expenditure including expenditure on major repair and maintenance in farm business,
(l) expenditure on normal repairs and maintenance of assets used in farm business.

Fixed capital formation in farm business is considered as constituted of all expenditure included under gross capital expenditure in farm business excepting those incurred for normal repair and maintenance of the existing assets and expenditure for purchase of land, land rights and livestock.

Expenditure incurred for purchase of fertilisers, improved seeds, pesticides, etc., are intermediate inputs and therefore, is not considered capital expenditure. It is necessary to point out here that in a number of studies on capital formation in Indian agriculture although purchase of land and land rights and expenditure incurred on them were not considered as expenditure on fixed capital formation in farm business, the expenditure incurred for the purchase of livestock and also on the purchase of process inputs, namely fertilisers, pesticides and improved seeds were considered as capital formation. This is conceptually incorrect and in this discussion we shall refrain from taking into account the expenditure on such inputs as either belonging to gross capital expenditure or to fixed capital formation. Now, before we start discussing the main theme of the nature of capital structure in Indian agriculture, it is worthwhile knowing what was the nature of the structure of capital investment during the period since when the process of change started.

Capital Structure in Agriculture Upto 1960-61

Taking as the starting point the period 1945-46 to 1950-51 since when the capital structure started taking new shape, the trend of capital investment made in Indian agriculture during the next decade is given below: The data presented in Table 3.1 have been taken from Tara Shukla's study on capital formation in Indian agriculture. It is observed that out of the total amount of Rs. 2321 crores, Rs. 3087 crores and Rs. 3704 crores spent respectively in 1945-46 to 1950-51, 1950-51 to 1955-56 and 1955-56 to 1960-61 for capital expenditure, i.e. on land, bullock, irrigation and implements respectively, the major share of investment made was on bullocks. The cash expenditure on other items, namely, land, irrigation and implements and tools trailed far behind that made on bullocks.

Table 3.1: Percentage distribution of gross capital formation in Indian agriculture (1945-46 to 1960-61)

Year	*Land*	*Bullock*	*Irrigation*	*Implement*	*Total (in crores)*
(1)	*(2)*	*(3)*	*(4)*	*(5)*	*(6)*
1945-46 to 1950-51	4.5	78.7	9.4	7.4	2321
1950-51 to 1955-56	14.0	61.4	19.4	5.2	3087
1955-56 to 1960-61	11.5	56.2	25.9	6.4	3704

Source: Tara Shukla: *Capital Formation in Indian Agriculture,* Varance, Bombay, p. 151.

It is clear that Indian agriculture, till 1960-61, i.e. even after one decade from the starting of planned investment programme on agriculture by the Central Government, remained tied to the traditional pattern of dependence mainly on human and animal labour. It could not be otherwise as despite large investment made through the first and the second plan towards building up major, medium and minor irrigation potential, for the private cultivators at large the situation had not become congenial enough either to fruitfully use the newly constructed irrigation potential or even to make use of the modern technological inputs for which heavy subsidies were offered by the governments. Perhaps, only a small section among the rich cultivators made some initial attempt for using the resource potential, or, make some headway in changing the structure of capital in farm business. This has been reflected in the aggregated information presented in Table 3.1. But nevertheless one could notice from the data the signal of change, as the proportion of expenditure on bullocks was seen to be sliding down and that on improvements on land, irrigation and implements gradually rising up, the tendency to spend on land as prime factor of agricultural production having remained almost unchanged notwithstanding. As for various reasons acquiring of more land was not always feasible, the more enterprising cultivators in all likelihood went for intensive use of the existing land by using irrigation water, improved seeds and fertiliser etc.

Impact of Central Intervention through Planned Investment in Agriculture

The nature and the extent of the initial impact of the massive governmental intervention through planned investment in agriculture for initiating change in the capital structure of the farm business can further be seen from the data presented in Table 3.2 which summarises the situation of gradual change till 1971-72.

The data shown in Table 3.2 makes it palpably clear that although the preference for capital expenditure on land and livestock remained upper most in the mind of cultivators in rural India at least till 1961-62, expenditures on land improvement and agricultural implements showed a tendency to rise in subsequent years. However, during the next decade, i.e. during 1961-62 to 1971-72 a slow but steady progress towards choosing the non-traditional path in agricultural production by at least a section of the cultivating community was clearly visible.

Table 3.2: Capital expenditure in farm business : Percentage proportion of different items of the total

Capital Items	*Percentage*		
	1951-52	*1961-62*	*1971-72*
(1)	*(2)*	*(3)*	*(4)*
1. Livestock	37.6	44.4	26.1
2. Land and land rights	17.1	19.7	18.4
3. Agricultural implements	8.7	11.4	19.2
4. Building and other land improvements	6.4	8.9	11.6
5. Digging of wells and development of other irrigation resources	11.0	8.0	12.2
6. Reclamation of land	3.6	2.9	2.2
7. Construction of farm buildings	4.0	2.9	5.0
8. Laying of orchards and plantation	4.0	1.1	4.6
9. Others	7.6	0.7	0.7
Total	100.0	100.0	100.0

Source: Report of the Committee of Direction, All-India Rural Credit Survey, Vol. I — The Survey Report, Part I, Reserve Bank of India, 1956, *Reserve Bank of India Bulletin*, June, 1965, *op. cit.*, pp. 846-47.

The data suggest that significant advance towards spending more on agricultural machineries and implements, on improvement of land, on digging of wells, tubewells, etc., for development of irrigation resources and even on diversification of agriculture, such as laying of orchards and plantation was attempted during this period. All these changes in the pattern of capital expenditure ushered-in, in the farm business, particularly on land improvement and irrigation and also perhaps on improved seeds, fertiliser and pesticides caused to bring about a marked change in the technique of cultivation. The resultant effect was a significant rise in agricultural production, particularly in the production of foodgrains, especially rice and wheat, a large quantity of which had to be imported till sixties. The official statistics of annual output for a few important crops available for 1950-56 (excepting for 1970-71) are shown in Table 3.3 for reference.

Table 3.3: Output of a few important agricultural commodities for the period 1951-56

Name of Crops	*Year*				*Percentage increase between 1950-51 & 1985-86*
	1950-51	*1960-81*	*1980-86*	*1985-86*	
(1)	*(2)*	*(3)*	*(4)*	*(5)*	*(6)*
1. Total foodgrains (m. tonne)	51	82	130	150	194
1.1 rice (m.t.)	21	35	54	64	205
1.2 wheat (m.t.)	6	11	36	47	683
2. Oil seeds (m.t.)	-	7	9	11	120
3. Sugarcane (m.t.)	57	110	154	172	202
4. Cotton (m. bales)	3	6	7	9	200
5. Jute (m.t.)	9	4	7	11	267

Source: Ministry of Agriculture, Annual Report (1986-87) and Economic Survey, 1986-87, Government of India.

Before we examine the data on various other aspects of capital expenditure and capital formation in Indian farm business and try to trace out the nature of the trend of their structural change, it is worthwhile looking into the extent of governmental investment in agriculture and irrigation made by way of outlays made in different five year plans, the pattern of the expenditure and how that helped to effect change in the capital structure of the farm business. In Table 3.4, the pattern of outlays in different five year plans is presented.

Table 3.4: Pattern of outlay in agriculture in the first and the subsequent plans

Plans	*Total plan outlay (in Rs. crores)*	*Public sector outlay in agri. (Rs. crores)*			*Total*	*Percentage of total outlay*
		Agriculture and community development	*Rural development and area programme*	*Irrigation and flood control*		
(1)	*(2)*	*(3)*	*(4)*	*(5)*	*(6)*	*(7)*
First Plan	1960	290	–	310	600	31
Second Plan	4600	530	–	420	950	20
Third Plan	8577	1080	–	665	1745	20
Annual Plan	6757	1167	–	457	1624	24
Fourth Plan	16160	–	–	–	3390	21
Fifth Plan	39300	4640	–	3440	8080	21
Sixth Plan	97500	12540	–	12160	24700	25
Seventh Plan	180000	10574	12218	16978	39770	22

Source: Various Plan Documents.

As development of irrigation potential which essentially meant building up of major, medium and minor irrigation infrastructure involved outlay of huge financial resources and the question of private cultivator's bearing that huge financial burden being inconceivable under the circumstances, the Government's massive intervention in this sector was necessary and inevitable. The data presented in Table 3.4 show that the bulk of the total plan outlay on agriculture and irrigation was allocated for irrigation work, the other part of the outlay was obviously spent on other items, namely, soil conservation and improvements, distribution of improved seeds, construction of other necessary infrastructure like construction of roads, irrigation canals, drainage facilities etc. Whatever may be the pattern of distribution of total plan outlay on agriculture and irrigation, the Centre's intervention for development of agriculture and the results obtained therefrom, in terms of increase of agricultural production undoubtedly opened up a new vista of development of Indian agriculture. The changed environment encouraged the cultivators to gradually shift from the traditional path of agricultural production and to break new grounds for moving towards modernisation of agriculture. Thus, they started using more and more on improved seeds, chemical fertilisers and pesticides and utilising irrigation potential built up as an outcome of the plan outlay. Government's initiative in the production of improved seeds and in granting heavy subsidy while distributing seeds and fertilisers to the cultivators helped them to generate additional incentive for more investment on these process inputs. Along with the investment on modern inputs, investment on fixed capital assets, namely, pumpsets, land improvement and agricultural machineries was also progressively increased. The nature and extent of development achieved in view of the plan outlay in agriculture and the changed behaviour of the cultivating community towards the application of modern inputs and machinery in their farm business is shown in Tables 3.5 and 3.6 respectively.

Table 3.5: Predicators of progress towards modernisation of agriculture

Indicators with unit of measurement	*Year*		
	1960-61	*1980-81*	*1986-87*
(1)	*(2)*	*(3)*	*(4)*
1. Irrigated area cumulative utilisation (m. hectares)	28	55	62
2. Consumption of pesticides (m. tonnes)	6	45	52
3. Area under high-yielding variety (m. hectares)	1.5	43	55
4. Consumption of chemicals fertiliser (m. tonnes)	0.3	5.5	8.7
5. Distribution of quality	–	2.5	5.5

Source: Department of Agriculture and Co-operation: Annual Report, 1986-87, Government of India.

Table 3.6: Indicators of progress in the use of machineries in farm business

Indicators with unit of measurement	*Year*			
	1961	*1970*	*1974*	*1980*
(1)	*(2)*	*(3)*	*(4)*	*(5)*
1. Tractors:				
Cumulative total (lakhs)	0.31	1.00	2.25	4.73
Per lakh hectares of gross cropped area (no.)	20	60	137	270
2. Oil Engines:				
Cumulative total (lakhs)	2.30	–	17.50	29.00
Per lakh hectares of gross cropped area (no.)	151	–	1063	1657
3. Irrigation pumps and electrically operated tubewells:				
Cumulative total (lakhs)	2.0	15.54	24.30	40.00
Per lakh hectares of gross cropped area (no.)	131	817	1486	2286
4. Consumption of power (kWh) of agriculture				
Per thousand hectares of gross cropped area	5.3	23.0	38.5	71.0
5. Gross cropped area (lakh hectares)	1528	1658	1646	1750

Source: CMIE : Basic Statistics Relating to Indian Economy, Vol. I, All India, October, 1980.

In India the debt and investment survey was conducted in 1981. The survey data in disaggregated form have not been published so far, by the RBI. The National Sample Survey Organisation, which collaborated in the said survey with RBI has published some data for the state and All India in one of their Reports (No. 334). This Report only presents the proportion of households reported to have incurred expenditure on any capital item (including or excluding items of tangible capital assets) and also the average amount of rupees spent per cultivator households in their farm business on such capital items.

Statewise Variation in the Pattern of Capital Expenditure and Capital Formation

The above mentioned survey data presented here in summarised form in two separate Tables 3.7 and 3.8 for different states and 'All India' provide a picture of the statewise variation of the pattern of capital expenditure and capital formation and add an additional dimension to the study of the trend of the changing pattern of capital expenditure and capital formation in farm business carried out by the cultivating households in rural India. From a perusal of the data presented in the two tables, the following broad conclusions can be drawn:

1. The timely financial 'push' given through the massive plan investment made in the first and the subsequent plans for development of agriculture and irrigation created such a favourable investment climate in the agricultural sector that in almost all the States, a sizeable large number of cultivating households engaged in farm business reported having incurred, in 1961-62, capital expenditure, a part of which was spent for fixed capital formation. However, in all the states, such euphoria for capital expenditure gradually declined over two subsequent decades. It might be noted that in 1981-82 on an average, about 40 per cent of the cultivating households engaged in farm business reported to have incurred capital expenditure, of course, with varying proportions in different states depending upon the peculiar situation obtaining in the respective states and about 16 per cent reported incurring of expenditure on capital formation.
2. The size of capital expenditure, which apart from expenditures on items of fixed capital also includes

other capital items, such as land, livestock and normal repair and maintenance, was observed to be higher in almost all states than the expenditure incurred on fixed capital formation alone. This pattern, however, varied from state to state. It becomes evident as the proportion of households reported to be incurring expenditure only on fixed capital was observed to be half or even less, in almost all the states, than the respective proportions of households reported to have incurred capital expenditure.

3. In so far as the pattern of capital expenditure and fixed capital formation obtaining in the different states in India is concerned, all the states of India can broadly be brought under two distinct groups. While in the states belonging to Group I, the beneficial effect of the government's effort for development of agriculture could bring out impressive results, in the Group II states, the perceived progress of the change in capital structure was rather slow and limping. The names of states classified under Group I and Group II are given below:

Groups	*Name of States*
(1)	*(2)*
I	Andhra Pradesh, Gujarat, Maharashtra, Karnataka, Jammu & Kashmir, Rajasthan, Punjab, Haryana, Tamil Nadu
II	Assam, Bihar, Kerala, Madhya Pradesh, Orissa, Uttar Pradesh, West Bengal

It is difficult to assign specific reasons for the observed difference in the pattern of trend of capital expenditure and capital formation in two groups of states unless we can look into other factors, such as, pattern of plan allocation for agriculture and irrigation in different states, and the respective condition of land, agriculture and irrigation.

The other institutional factors, such as, the system of land tenure and pattern of size distribution of land and other infrastructural factors etc., of which one important factor is the nature of access of the cultivators to the credit facilities provided for by the government or other financial institution. All the above factors considered either separately or all of them taken together influence the decision-making of the cultivator households in regard to the change of technology and/or the change of capital structure in their respective farm business. But it is difficult to pin-point the most crucial factor among them which ultimately determine the decision-making of the cultivator households for incurring expenditure on fixed or other capital items. In fact, in all probability, a cluster of factors working together rather than a single factor is responsible.

4. Although, both for capital expenditure and capital formation, the average amount of expenditure per household, all of which are given in current prices, has been observed to have taken a rising trend over the two decades between 1961-62 and 1981-82, the extent of real increase may not be that significant because, during the same period, the prices of all commodities also spiralled very high.

With regard to the trend of the capital investment pattern in private farm business, we have so far examined the data on capital expenditure for the period 1950-51 to 1971-72 incurred on a few broad capital items for the country as a whole (See Table 3.2). Now almost similar information separately for a few major states relating only to 1961-62 and 1971-72 are presented in Table 3.9. While admitting that the data are inadequate in the sense that for subsequent period we have no information to present in view of their non-availability, whatever data are available are presented on the presumption that the trend of the pattern does not suggest that in the subsequent years a drastic change is going to take place and the conclusions derived from the given data would not thus be altogether irrelevant and proved invalid.

Table 3.7: Fixed capital formation by cultivator households in farm business by states

States	*Amount spent on capital formation per cultivating household reporting capital formation (in Rs. 000)*			*Percentage of cultivator households reporting fixed capital formation*		
	1961-62	*1971-72*	*1981-82*	*1961-62*	*1971-72*	*1981-82*
(1)	*(2)*	*(3)*	*(4)*	*(5)*	*(6)*	*(7)*
Andhra Pradesh	255.04	311.55	1145.00	17.35	9.60	16.41
Assam	89.79	118.06	270.00	25.16	22.11	19.01
Bihar	56.94	102.25	413.00	25.06	17.16	16.50
Gujarat	335.26	561.72	1892.00	22.79	26.01	17.03
Jammu & Kashmir	276.58	141.13	440.00	27.39	29.45	25.75
Karnataka	243.96	312.45	1147.00	34.69	31.95	17.45
Kerala	81.36	235.94	944.00	27.41	9.68	14.31
Madhya Pradesh	84.26	269.50	691.00	22.09	20.32	21.89
Maharashtra	255.26	439.31	1396.00	22.05	18.43	21.85
Orissa	68.40	75.22	140.00	35.99	22.44	26.24
Punjab } Haryana	111.00	1118.26	3134.00	45.30	46.03	29.23
Rajasthan	165.35	305.87	1794.00	16.44	29.15	13.04
Tamil Nadu	269.19	535.87	1250.00	22.49	13.93	13.19
Uttar Pradesh	79.17	316.16	1438.00	25.22	15.69	12.12
West Bengal	49.32	105.76	401.00	16.77	24.25	13.52
All India	140.24	319.27	1786.00	23.32	19.33	16.07

Sources:(i) Reserve Bank of India, Statistical Tables on Capital Expenditure and Capital Formation of Rural Households during the year ending 30th June, 1962 and 1972.

(ii) NSSO Report No. 334: Broad Feature of Capital Expenditure incurred by Rural and Urban Households during 1981-82.

Table 3.8: Proportion of cultivator households reporting gross capital expenditure and average amount of gross capital expenditure per cultivating household in farm business in 1961-62, 1971-72 and 1981-82

States	*Percentage of cultivator households reporting gross capital expenditure in*			*Average amount of gross capital expenditure in farm business per cultivator household in (Rs. 000)*		
	1961-62	*1971-72*	*1981-82*	*1961-62*	*1971-72*	*1981-82*
(1)	*(2)*	*(3)*	*(4)*	*(5)*	*(6)*	*(7)*
Andhra Pradesh	46.30	27.35	48.49	396.22	466.20	1123
Assam	69.61	41.91	27.89	147.00	251.51	467
Bihar	73.49	37.23	35.17	95.52	196.73	443
Gujarat	64.35	63.93	45.48	314.01	583.58	1174
Jammu & Kashmir	49.62	71.10	70.50	214.47	217.20	851
Karnataka	74.65	58.48	49.80	364.29	614.73	1608
Kerala	65.21	39.84	43.69	142.92	299.67	1246
Madhya Pradesh	63.42	59.94	60.15	176.71	373.08	596
Maharashtra	59.88	50.00	56.16	237.53	493.91	1108
Orissa	56.07	50.28	47.64	137.51	149.48	331
Punjab	* 80.14	71.23	51.46	* 360.56	1760.11	2791
Haryana		62.41	57.41		1366.27	1984
Rajasthan	58.16	57.55	25.29	313.59	457.51	1905
Tamil Nadu	51.64	39.90	32.55	364.29	553.77	1240
Uttar Pradesh	83.19	51.93	65.15	162.69	360.83	724
West Bengal	65.53	52.90	42.25	91.15	249.03	443
All India	66.68	48.60	39.11	209.14	422.96	913

Sources: (i) Reserve Bank of India, Statistical Tables on Capital Expenditure and Capital Formation of Rural Households during the year ending 30th June, 1962 & 1972.

Based: All India Debt Investment Survey 1961-62 & 1971-72.

(ii) NSSO Report No. 334: Broad Features of Capital Expenditure incurred by Rural and Urban Households during 1981-82.

(iii)* 1961-62 figures are for undivided Punjab which includes Haryana.

It may be observed from the data shown in Table 3.9, that in all most all the states, of the total amount of capital investment made in farm business, proportionately more was spent on building up private irrigation infrastructure, namely wells, tubewells, and other irrigation equipment and on purchasing agricultural equipment both of traditional and modern variety in 1971-72 than to that reported in 1961-62. Also it is observed that for the states categorised by us as Group I, the respective proportion of shares of investment for improvement and construction of wells and other irrigation resources and also for agricultural equipments and machineries, particularly those of modern variety, are distinctly higher compared to the corresponding shares observed for states categorised as Group II. It can generally be stated that government's adoption of new agricultural strategy for which massive funding for agriculture and irrigation was made through different five-year plans had its salutary effect in inducing the cultivator households to change the capital structure of their farm business in almost all states in the country, of course, depending on the varying conditions of agriculture prevailing in different states, the size and shape of the change was different, as the reported share of capital investment, particularly for building up irrigation resources and for acquiring modern agricultural implements, was observed to be proportionately higher in a large number of states, compared to the reported shares for the identical group of capital items for the few other remaining states. But the situation described above does not necessarily mean that all sections of the cultivator households in different states behaved in a similar fashion and there was a general upward shift all along the line of the capital investment in rural farm business and expenditure on the different components of the fixed capital structure also recorded an uniform upward rise.

Variation of Capital Structure According to the Size of Household Asset-Holding

Now, we shall address ourselves to the question as to which section of the cultivator households engaged in rural farm business could take advantage of the successive plan outlays for agriculture and irrigation and could utilise the irrigation and other infrastructural facilities provided for, by the government by fruitfully using their individual savings or by obtaining credit from institutional or non-institutional source for augmenting the capital investment in their farm business. The published results of the All India Debt and Investment Survey conducted in 1971-72 provides some clues for giving probable answers to such questions.

Presuming that the value of household asset-holding is a fair indicator of the economic level of a rural or cultivator households, it may not be unjustified to consider, in the absence of household income data, the value of household asset-holding as a suitable proxy for household income. In Table 3.10, the distribution of cultivator households in farm business by size-class of asset-holding and for the households belonging to each asset-holding group, the share of each type of capital items of the total value of fixed capital formation is presented. Taking the households belonging to each of the asset-holding group upto Rs. 5,000, Rs. 5,000-15,000, Rs. 15,000-30,000 and Rs. 30,000 and above respectively as low-income, moderate-income, middle-income and high-income households, four distinct capital investment patterns for four different sets of household emerge out of data shown in Table 3.10. The characteristics of the respective capital investment pattern are described below:

(a) In the low-income group, which constituted about 19 per cent of total number of rural cultivator households, major portion of the value of total capital investment made in a year was apportioned for acquiring or bringing into use for cultivation of new areas of land and their improvements, only a small portion for either construction of improvements of irrigation resources and whatever remained of the total amount was used for acquiring only the traditional types of agricultural implements. The capital investment pattern adopted in agricultural operation in this group of households was evidently of the traditional nature.

Table 3.9: Percentage share of individual items of fixed capital formation in farm business

State	Period	Bunding and other land improvement	Orchards and plantation (new additions)	Wells	Other irrigation resources	Purchase of agricultural implements		Farm houses, burns etc.	Others
						Traditional	Improved		
(1)	(2)	(3)	(4)	(5)	(6)	(7)	(8)	(9)	(10)
Andhra Pradesh	1961-62	34.13	0.13	25.66	0.58	11.98	21.01	6.51	–
	1971-72	19.70	0.57	38.40	0.92	24.92	11.61	3.60	0.30
Assam	1961-62	67.30	3.53	1.85	8.23	2.14	0.31	14.14	2.50
	1971-72	30.82	15.94	2.51	1.36	10.07	7.53	31.29	0.48
Bihar	1961-62	25.66	0.92	24.91	9.81	20.54	6.05	12.11	–
	1971-72	27.76	3.24	12.14	4.74	18.91	26.83	5.15	1.23
Gujarat	1961-62	16.32	0.23	16.95	2.15	20.94	33.71	9.38	0.32
	1971-72	6.35	0.23	23.62	4.68	30.58	24.51	7.54	2.49
Jammu & Kashmir	1961-62	20.73	6.03	9.82	0.38	0.97	0.32	61.75	–
	1971-72	16.46	8.16	0.70	0.88	22.40	0.68	48.49	1.78
Karnataka	1961-62	35.33	9.70	25.92	0.50	13.86	7.52	5.81	1.36
	1971-72	34.16	3.33	17.54	0.88	16.93	19.22	5.14	2.80
Kerala	1961-62	38.68	23.16	2.46	7.64	9.02	6.81	8.91	3.32
	1971-72	36.79	13.03	10.03	2.58	12.08	13.68	10.04	1.17
Madhya Pradesh	1961-62	40.30	0.03	33.26	–	11.82	4.53	8.07	1.99
	1971-72	18.12	0.04	36.18	4.22	16.71	15.28	8.48	0.97

(Contd.)

Table 3.9 *(Contd.)*

(1)	(2)	(3)	(4)	(5)	(6)	(7)	(8)	(9)	(10)
Maharashtra	1961-62	36.73	1.20	32.97	2.45	6.08	12.98	7.21	0.38
	1971-72	19.28	4.29	33.64	2.40	21.12	7.61	11.26	0.40
Orissa	1961-62	83.76	0.04	3.16	0.46	8.52	0.05	3.93	0.07
	1971-72	53.66	8.91	4.04	2.12	15.54	4.28	8.52	2.93
Punjab & Haryana	1961-62	17.92	0.40	12.32	4.71	22.42	24.42	17.83	0.03
Punjab	1971-72	6.62	0.07	7.85	13.69	21.96	33.45	15.85	0.51
Haryana	1971-72	11.11	0.43	16.77	10.28	18.98	29.28	12.63	0.52
Rajasthan	1961-62	11.12	0.22	41.14	4.40	23.56	11.47	7.77	0.32
	1971-72	11.94	0.06	30.58	1.10	29.10	20.14	6.24	0.33
Tamil Nadu	1961-62	21.25	1.09	34.51	0.44	12.35	24.48	3.08	2.80
	1971-72	14.08	0.37	31.66	4.65	17.50	26.59	4.45	0.70
Uttar Pradesh	1961-62	31.36	2.54	21.66	4.52	17.64	8.77	13.32	0.19
	1971-72	7.44	0.74	16.53	11.72	27.78	21.92	13.74	0.13
West Bengal	1961-62	25.66	4.68	2.16	1.59	15.99	4.22	43.36	2.34
	1971-72	30.80	4.05	5.77	3.06	29.26	14.72	11.29	1.03
All India	1961-62	32.29	2.76	24.05	2.40	13.79	14.76	9.12	0.98
	1971-72	16.55	1.80	21.14	5.99	22.39	20.80	10.28	1.08

Source: Reserve Bank of India, Statistical Tables on Capital Expenditure and Capital Formation of Rural Households during the year ending 30th June, 1972.

Table 3.10: Share of holdings in each type of capital item of the total fixed capital expenditure for each group

Asset-group (in rupees)	Percentage of households	Total	Fixed capital formation in farm business: Reclamation of land: New land brought under cultivation	Reclamation of land: Land temporary out of cultivation	Bunding other land implements: Major alterations and additions	Bunding other land implements: New constructions	Orchards and plantations (new additions)	Wells: Major alterations	Wells: New constructions	Other irrigation resources: Major alterations	Other irrigation resources: New construction	Purchase of agricultural implements and machinery: Traditional type	Purchase of agricultural implements and machinery: Improved type	Farm house burns and cattle sheds: Major alterations	Farm house burns and cattle sheds: New additions	Farm house burns and cattle sheds: New constructions	Others
(1)	(2)	(3)	(4)	(5)	(6)	(7)	(8)	(9)	(10)	(11)	(12)	(13)	(14)	(15)	(16)	(17)	(18)
Upto 500	2.04	100.0	16.16	5.04	12.91	12.03	12.13	-	-	-	1.04	29.50	1.50	5.20	-	4.49	-
500-1000	3.67	100.0	23.01	2.12	4.07	6.98	1.09	2.96	23.72	0.75	1.77	29.35	0.46	0.56	-	0.30	2.89
1000-2500	12.79	100.0	20.45	5.70	7.66	1.23	5.98	0.20	10.64	0.70	2.74	25.94	1.55	3.59	0.16	10.69	2.78
2500-5000	18.16	100.0	8.97	4.93	8.84	5.32	5.12	4.38	13.27	0.04	2.13	29.46	3.37	1.90	1.90	7.32	2.04
5000-10000	23.13	100.0	6.36	5.01	5.71	9.37	1.75	3.48	18.24	0.15	1.83	31.36	5.76	1.37	0.58	7.02	1.51
10000-15000	12.72	100.0	4.68	4.17	4.72	4.90	1.55	4.82	15.77	0.45	3.72	31.93	11.30	1.16	0.89	7.53	2.43
15000-20000	7.60	100.0	3.39	3.68	2.15	2.76	1.90	7.89	22.65	0.05	6.60	20.99	19.36	0.51	0.67	6.32	0.57
20000-30000	8.29	100.0	5.41	2.33	6.12	5.26	1.54	5.96	20.95	0.98	4.30	19.55	17.30	1.23	0.59	8.06	0.42
30000-50000	6.43	100.0	6.10	1.86	2.47	7.88	1.96	4.43	19.10	0.78	6.76	19.26	17.23	0.65	1.17	9.78	0.64
50000-100000	3.90	100.0	4.98	0.77	3.72	2.80	1.18	5.09	11.72	1.36	3.50	20.31	31.68	1.05	2.31	9.21	0.31
100000 & above	1.27	100.0	3.47	0.63	2.96	2.57	1.78	4.02	1.49	1.26	9.02	19.23	32.95	0.65	1.35	6.55	2.08
Total	100.0	100.0	5.30	2.31	3.99	4.95	1.80	4.91	16.23	0.81	5.18	22.37	20.80	0.98	1.25	8.05	1.08

Source: Reserve Bank of India, Statistical Tables on Capital Expenditure and Capital Formation of Rural Households during the year ending 30th June, 1972.

Based: All India Debt Investment Survey 1971-72.

(b) Among the cultivator households belonging to the moderate-income group, a slight departure from traditional path was noticed. Emphasis laid here was less on land and its improvements and more on irrigation resources and traditional types of agricultural implements. Very little was spent on acquiring improved agricultural machineries and implements. Quite probably this group of households attached more importance on intensive cultivation and change of cropping pattern having made use of the irrigation potential built-up by government that created favourable condition for the use of new technological inputs, such as, improved seeds, fertilisers, etc.

(c) In the middle income group, a clearer pattern of gradual shift from the traditional to modern path of agricultural production was observed. This group reported to have allocated the bulk of their capital investment for two items, namely, expansion of irrigation resources and purchase of machinery and implements. It should be noted that of the total share of capital investment for machinery and implements, the share of traditional types of implements was observed to be higher than that of the modern variety although, compared to the corresponding allocated share of the moderate income of the households, the share of capital investment for modern or improved varieties of machinery or implements was observed to be higher in this group of households.

(d) It may be observed that households belonging to the high-income group allocated more than 70 per cent of the total capital investment mainly for two items, namely, building of irrigation resources and agricultural machinery and implements having allocated about 25 to 30 per cent of the total capital investment for building up irrigation resources. Again of the total allocation made for machinery and implements, a larger share was observed to have been allocated for improved varieties rather than for traditional varieties.

It will not thus be a speculation to conclude that from the plan investment for the purpose of bringing about technological change in the agriculture, the derived benefit was accrued mostly by the relatively well-to-do section of the cultivator households. But concurrently it should be acknowledged that the new agricultural strategy ushered-in by the government since sixties brought about in general, a perceptible change of investment climate in agricultural economy. The middle and the upper lair of the cultivating community, though gradually adapted themselves favourably to the changing situation to take some positive steps towards adopting modern path of agricultural development instead of sticking to the traditional path, they constituted only about 27 per cent of the total number of cultivator households, whereas, the other 73 per cent still remained tied-up to the traditional path and in so far as building up their own irrigation resources and in acquiring of improved varieties of agricultural machinery and implements were concerned they rather took a conservative attitude. In rural India, the former group, therefore, clearly stands out as the emerging entrepreneurial class engaged in farm business.

However, the overall all India trend of the pattern of capital structure in farm business presented above may not hold good for the different states as the factors which influence the supply and demand of the different capital items are different in different states. In this connection, the statistical tables released by the RBI on the All India Debt and Investment Survey carried out in 1971-72 showing the proportion of households reporting expenditure on different items of fixed capital and the percentage share of the value of different items of fixed capital of the total value of all fixed capital items acquired by household belonging to different household asset-holding group may be carefully looked into. Because of the bulky size, those tables are not presented here.

An analysis of the data presented in those tables will show that, although the traditional path has not been altogether discarded in anyone of the states, the proportion of households pursuing traditional path is reported to be higher than the corresponding proportion adopting the modern path in Bihar,

Orissa, Assam, Madhya Pradesh, Kerala and West Bengal and the proportion of cultivator households reported to be showing increasing tendency to adopt the modern path is higher than the corresponding proportion following the traditional path in Punjab, Haryana, Gujarat, Maharashtra, Karnataka and Tamil Nadu. It is generally believed that only the relatively richer section of the cultivators are the real beneficiaries of the plan investment in agriculture who venture adoption of modern path of development in their farm business using both modern technological inputs, building up their own irrigation resources and improved varieties of machinery and implement. The survey data proves that such popular notion has a factual basis. It is observed that while in the first group of states (listed above) the so-called richer section has been found to be proportionately less, in the second Group (listed above) the proportion of the richer section is higher.

But, why only a few geographical regions and also only a small section within each geographical region could make better use of the massive government investment in agriculture? We must find out an answer to this important question.

On the basis of a careful examination of the available data we feel inclined to conclude that for such lopsided progress in bringing about change of capital structure in agriculture, among other factors, the following two institutional factors are considered most important:

(a) skewed size distribution pattern of land either owned or operated by cultivator households in rural areas,
(b) limited opportunity of the credit facilities provided for by government and other financial institutions for cultivator households having small holding size and meagre availability of credit facilities even from non-institutional sources for these small holder households.

Size Distribution of Land and its Effect on Capital Structure in Agriculture

Let us first look into the size distribution pattern of land holdings in rural area. A set of data compiled from official sources is presented in Tables 3.11 to 3.14. Briefly the above data may be interpreted as follows:

(a) Till 1980-81, large areas of land remain concentrated among a small proportion of rural households while a large proportion of them own or operate a relatively smaller area of total land.

(b) The number of marginal holdings (below 1 hectare) constitute about 56 per cent of the total number of operational holding enumerated in 1980-81 and they cover a little over 12 per cent of the total land area under different productive operation. For the same year, the proportion of total number of medium and large holdings (4 hectares and above) enumerated was a little over 11 per cent of the total number of operational holding and they cover more than 52 per cent of the total area of holdings. It may also be noted that whereas the average size of marginal holdings is only 0.39 hectares, the average size of the medium (4 to 10 hectares) and large holdings (10 hectares and above) is 5.9 hectares and 17.2 hectares respectively. Obviously some of the individual marginal holdings are bound to be too tiny for agricultural operation and the application therein of traditional technique along with employment of household labour perhaps is considered to be the only viable step. The question of building up of costly irrigation resources and acquiring improved agricultural implements in such a situation did not occur to them as such a venture perhaps would have been uneconomic.

(c) The state-wise data on average size of operational holdings facilitate classification of the states under two broad groups. While in the first group (Group I) the range of the average holding size is between 1.9 to 4.4 hectares, in the second group (Group II) the corresponding range of the average holding size is between 0.4 hectares to 1.6 hectares. It may be noted that barring one or two states, the states classified earlier in this chapter under Group I also come under the Group I state now categorised according to average size of land-holding and there the capital structure in agriculture is observed to be undergoing gradual transformation through progressive application of modern technique. In the Group II states, on the other hand, the pace of such transformation is observed to be slow and halting.

In view of the typical pattern of size distribution of land owned or operated obtaining in rural areas, it is understandable why modernisation of agriculture remains restricted to only a small section of the rural cultivator households. And since the change from the present to a more favourable pattern of the size distribution of land is not likely to come about very soon, the prospect of rapid progress in changing the capital structure of Indian agriculture within a reasonably short span of time is not likely to be bright.

Table 3.11: Percentage proportion of households, area owned by size-class of ownership holding and year

	1953-54		*1961-62*		*1971-72*	
Size-group of ownership holding	*No. of house-holds*	*Area owned (acres)*	*No. of house-holds*	*Area owned (acres)*	*No. of house-holds*	*Area owned (acres)*
(1)	*(2)*	*(3)*	*(4)*	*(5)*	*(6)*	*(7)*
Marginal (below 1 acre)	31	1	37	2	44	2
Small (1-5 acre)	36	15	35	18	34	23
Medium (5-15 acres)	23	31	20	35	17	36
Big (15-50 acres)	9	35	7	34	5	31
Large (50 & above)	1	18	1	11	-	8
Total	100	100	100	100	100	100

Source: NSSO Reports : No. 36, No. 144 and No. 215.

Table 3.12: Percentage of number of operational holdings and area of operational holdings in India by holding size-class by year

Size category	*Percentage of total number*			*Percentage of total area*		
	1970-71	*1976-77*	*1980-81*	*1970-71*	*1976-77*	*1980-81*
(1)	*(2)*	*(3)*	*(4)*	*(5)*	*(6)*	*(7)*
Marginal (below 1 hectare)	51.0	54.6	56.6	9.0	10.7	12.1
Small (1 to 4 hectare)	33.9	32.4	32.0	30.4	32.7	35.3
Medium (4 to 10 hectares)	11.2	10.0	9.1	29.7	30.4	29.7
Large (10 hectares & above)	3.9	3.0	2.3	30.9	26.2	22.9
Total	100.0	100.0	100.0	100.0	100.0	100.0

Source: Agricultural Situation in India, October, 1981 and August, 1985.

Table 3.13: Average size of holding by size-class of holding and year

Size category	*Average size in hectares*		
	1970-71	*1976-77*	*1980-81*
(1)	*(2)*	*(3)*	*(4)*
Marginal (below 1 hectare)	0.40	0.39	0.39
Small (1 to 2 hectares)	1.44	1.42	1.43
Small medium (2 to 4 hectares)	2.81	2.78	2.77
Medium (4 to 10 hectares)	6.08	6.04	5.98
Large (10 hectares & above)	18.09	17.53	17.24
Total	2.28	2.00	1.82

Source: Compiled from All-India Report on Agricultural Census (1976-77) and Agricultural Situation in India, August, 1985.

Table 3.14: Average size of an operational holding in India

States	*Average size in hectares*		
	1970-71	*1976-77*	*1980-81*
(1)	*(2)*	*(3)*	*(4)*
Rajasthan	5.46	4.85	4.44
Maharashtra	4.28	3.66	2.95
Gujarat	4.11	3.71	3.45
Madhya Pradesh	4.00	3.60	3.42
Haryana	3.77	3.58	3.54
Karnataka	3.20	2.98	2.73
Punjab	2.89	2.74	3.79
Andhra Pradesh	2.51	2.34	1.87
All India	2.28	2.00	1.82
Orissa	1.89	1.60	1.59
Bihar	1.50	1.10	0.99
Assam	1.47	1.37	1.36
Tamil Nadu	1.45	1.25	1.07
West Bengal	1.20	0.99	0.94
Uttar Pradesh	1.16	1.05	1.01
Kerala	0.57	0.49	0.43

Source: Ministry of Agriculture, Agricultural Situation in India, October, 1981.

Inadequacy of Credit Facilities

The other important factor, which is considered to have hindered investment at increasing rate by cultivator households on modern capital inputs and fixed capital items for their farm business, is the inadequate availability of credit facilities to cater to their need for cash for such specific purposes. Although, since sixties there has been significant expansion of credit facilities provided for by government directly and also indirectly through co-operative societies, land mortgage banks and commercial banks, all sections of the cultivator households have not been able to utilise such facilities either for changing the technique of production or in improving the capital structure of their farm even when other complimentary factors have been found to be favourable to venture taking such a forward step.

We shall make an attempt to find out why some sections of the cultivator households are landed into such an impasse and shall try to identify the probable reasons. But in this endeavour we are rather handicapped as the required data for such analysis with sufficient disaggregation and also for a number of time points are not available. However, for a few relevant aspects of indebtedness of cultivator households official data are available. The only source in this regard is the results of the All-India Debt and Investment Surveys conducted in 1961-62 and 1971-72 published by RBI and some aggregated results of the same survey conducted in 1981-82 and published by the NSSO. For the later years we have made use of some stray information available in different official publication though mostly they are aggregated data on a very few characteristics of indebtedness. A set of data is presented in Tables 3.15 to 3.18, for some characteristics, only All-India picture is shown and for others, data are available both at the All-India and the State levels.

Farmer's need for cash to carry on their cultivation is well-known. They obtain cash through loans advanced both by institutional and non-institutional sources. They need this financial support for short, medium and long period depending on their need for cultivation as well as their households consumption need. Generally, short-term loans are used for purchase of capital inputs and to meet the household consumption need and the medium and long-term loans are taken to purchase tangible capital assets including purchase of additional land and also for paying off old debts. Usually, short-term loans are repaid after harvest and for medium or long-term loans they have to abide by some stringent conditionalities such as, hypothecation of household assets etc., which for poorer section of the cultivators becomes sometimes difficult to abide by as they possess very little of such assets.

These sections of cultivators are considered as either having no, or, very poor credit worthiness. Non-institutional or private sources of credit, such as, moneylenders, traders etc., dominated the credit market till 1951-52 as the flow of institutional credit was meagre and neither to the government nor to the

Table 3.15: Cash debt owned to different credit agencies by cultivators—State-wise (As on June 30)

(Percentage)

States	Government		Co-op. society/ Co-op. bank		Commercial bank		Insurance*		Provident fund*		Landlord	
	1961	1971	1961	1971	1961	1971	1961	1971	1961	1971	1961	1971
(1)	(2)	(3)	(4)	(5)	(6)	(7)	(8)	(9)	(10)	(11)	(12)	(13)
1. Andhra Pradesh	2.3	2.5	7.2	10.5	0.2	2.2		Neg.		0.1	0.2	15.3
2. Assam	12.0	24.3	9.5	10.9	–	–		0.1		0.4	0.9	3.2
3. Bihar	5.3	6.3	1.0	4.8	–	0.4		–		0.1	–	16.9
4. Gujarat	5.9	5.8	29.6	42.5	–	3.5		Neg.		Neg.	0.2	2.3
5. Haryana**	–	4.9	–	23.1	–	2.7		–		–	–	–
6. Himachal Pradesh*	–	5.4	–	17.6	–	1.1		–		–	–	3.4
7. Jammu & Kashmir	0.1	12.5	6.8	7.9	0.2	0.1		–		Neg.	3.6	1.1
8. Karnataka	3.2	8.9	12.8	16.7	0.2	5.0		0.1		Neg.	0.9	14.1
9. Kerala	5.8	4.8	9.2	26.1	3.2	13.5		0.2		0.5	3.0	2.8
10. Madhya Pradesh	7.5	4.2	17.7	27.8	0.1	1.2		0.2		0.1	0.4	4.4
11. Maharashtra	24.8	12.0	34.0	57.3	–	1.4		Neg.		–	1.0	2.1
12. Orissa*	15.7	9.2	16.0	22.1	–	0.8		–		0.4	1.3	10.3
13. Punjab**	4.6	6.9	8.3	32.0	–	4.9		–		0.1	8.3	11.0
14. Rajasthan	4.5	3.9	2.8	5.3	–	0.6		Neg.		–	0.4	2.5
15. Tamil Nadu	3.4	6.2	10.7	16.2	1.3	1.8		0.1		0.1	0.3	10.5
16. Uttar Pradesh	3.3	9.5	11.0	14.9	0.2	1.6		0.7		0.4	–	6.3
17. West Bengal	25.0	16.3	4.7	15.1	–	1.3		–		0.3	0.7	3.7
18. All India	6.7	7.1	11.4	22.0	0.3	2.4		0.1		0.1	0.9	8.1

Note: * Data not available for 1961. ** Figures shown against Punjab for 1961 are inclusive of Haryana. Neg. = Negligible.

(Contd.)

Table 3.15: (*Contd.*)

Credit Agencies (*Percentage*)

States	Agriculturist money lender		Professional money lender		Trade		Relative/friend		Others		Total	
	1961	1971	1961	1971	1961	1971	1961	1971	1961	1971	1961	1971
(1)	(2)	(3)	(4)	(5)	(6)	(7)	(8)	(9)	(10)	(11)	(12)	(13)
1. Andhra Pradesh	66.5	36.0	9.7	9.7	9.7	7.9	1.7	12.1	2.5	3.7	100.0	100.0
2. Assam	39.6	12.5	14.7	7.6	6.9	8.3	12.1	26.6	4.3	6.1	100.0	100.0
3. Bihar	76.7	46.5	10.5	9.3	2.3	1.3	2.6	12.8	1.6	1.6	100.0	100.0
4. Gujarat	10.7	7.4	7.4	4.8	15.5	16.8	14.7	15.1	16.0	1.8	100.0	100.0
5. Haryana**	–	19.8	–	21.0	–	6.2	–	10.8	–	1.1	100.0	100.0
6. Himachal Pradesh*	–	27.6	–	10.7	–	2.9	–	31.2	–	0.1	100.0	100.0
7. Jammu & Kashmir	7.1	1.0	5.4	10.7	32.2	32.5	24.1	32.2	20.5	1.0	100.0	100.0
8. Karnataka	66.0	26.5	1.9	12.6	6.5	5.6	3.9	8.7	4.6	1.8	100.0	100.0
9. Kerala	17.3	7.4	4.9	8.5	4.9	4.9	12.0	22.5	39.7	8.8	100.0	100.0
10. Madhya Pradesh	32.3	19.3	29.9	25.6	9.0	10.5	2.0	5.2	1.1	1.5	100.0	100.0
11. Maharashtra	14.2	5.8	6.5	3.2	3.7	5.4	7.5	11.5	8.2	1.3	100.0	100.0
12. Orissa	23.1	24.6	32.9	15.2	5.5	1.6	2.2	12.5	3.3	3.3	100.0	100.0
13. Punjab**	50.7	9.3	11.6	5.8	2.0	12.3	10.4	14.8	4.1	2.9	100.0	100.0
14. Rajasthan	30.1	27.3	36.5	21.4	15.0	21.8	4.3	12.6	6.4	4.6	100.0	100.0
15. Tamil Nadu	65.1	31.2	7.2	13.1	4.9	4.7	2.2	13.3	4.9	2.8	100.0	100.0
16. Uttar Pradesh	43.9	25.6	20.0	22.2	4.4	4.3	7.2	12.6	10.0	2.4	100.0	100.0
17. West Bengal	33.8	12.5	6.8	15.6	10.8	9.4	9.4	24.1	8.8	1.7	100.0	100.0
18. All India	48.1	23.0	13.8	13.1	7.1	8.4	5.2	13.1	6.5	2.6	100.0	100.0

Note: * Data not available for 1961. ** Figures shown against Punjab for 1961 are inclusive of Haryana.
Neg. = Negligible.

Source: All India Debt and Investment Survey, 1971-72, Reserve Bank of India, Bombay.

Table 3.16: Proportion of cultivator households reporting cash debt according to credit agencies—State-wise (as on June 30)

(*Percentage*)

States	*Government*		*Co-op. society/ Co-op. bank*		*Commercial bank*		*Insurance**		*Provident fund**		*Landlord*	
	1961	*1971*	*1961*	*1971*	*1961*	*1971*	*1961*	*1971*	*1961*	*1971*	*1961*	*1971*
(1)	*(2)*	*(3)*	*(4)*	*(5)*	*(6)*	*(7)*	*(8)*	*(9)*	*(10)*	*(11)*	*(12)*	*(13)*
1. Andhra Pradesh	4.9	2.4	7.4	5.2	0.1	0.6		0.1		0.1	0.5	9.8
2. Assam	5.2	2.1	5.8	3.1	–	–		Neg.		0.1	0.1	0.9
3. Bihar	5.4	4.0	2.2	2.8	–	Neg.		–		0.1	0.2	6.3
4. Gujarat	2.8	3.6	16.3	22.4	Neg.	1.3		0.1		Neg.	0.3	1.8
5. Haryana**	–	2.6	–	8.9	–	0.4		–		–	–	4.8
6. Himachal Pradesh*	–	1.6	–	8.6	–	0.3		–		–	–	1.6
7. Jammu & Kashmir	0.2	3.3	6.4	8.4	0.1	Neg.		–		0.1	0.9	0.6
8. Karnataka	2.9	4.2	14.0	9.9	0.2	1.1		Neg.		Neg.	1.1	11.2
9. Kerala	2.8	1.2	7.5	11.4	3.3	3.6		0.1		0.4	3.6	1.9
10. Madhya Pradesh	5.1	1.8	14.3	13.3	–	0.3		Neg.		0.1	0.3	2.8
11. Maharashtra	11.1	13.2	24.7	30.9	0.1	0.5		0.1		–	0.7	2.2
12. Orissa	5.6	2.8	5.0	6.7	–	0.2		–		0.1	0.4	3.2
13. Punjab**	7.9	4.2	16.4	24.6	–	1.3		–		0.2	4.4	4.1
14. Rajasthan	4.4	5.0	5.8	6.5	–	0.2		Neg.		–	0.2	1.4
15. Tamil Nadu	5.1	4.7	12.1	10.6	1.2	1.0		0.1		0.1	0.7	8.7
16. Uttar Pradesh	2.0	2.8	9.7	6.1	Neg.	0.2		Neg.		0.1	0.1	3.7
17. West Bengal	16.4	9.3	3.7	7.8	Neg.	0.4		–		0.2	0.8	2.3
18. All India	3.3	4.3	9.9	9.8	0.2	0.5		Neg.		0.1	0.6	4.5

Note: * Data not available for 1961.
** Figures shown against Punjab for 1961 are inclusive of Haryana. Neg. = Negligible.

(*Contd.*)

Table 3.16: (*Contd.*)

(Percentage)

States	*Credit Agencies*											
	Agriculturist moneylender		*Professional moneylender*		*Trade*		*Relative/ friend*		*Others*		*Total*	
	1961	*1971*	*1961*	*1971*	*1961*	*1971*	*1961*	*1971*	*1961*	*1971*	*1961*	*1971*
(1)	*(2)*	*(3)*	*(4)*	*(5)*	*(6)*	*(7)*	*(8)*	*(9)*	*(10)*	*(11)*	*(12)*	*(13)*
1. Andhra Pradesh	42.5	20.5	8.2	6.1	8.1	7.1	2.7	9.0	2.9	2.3	59.4	53.4
2. Assam	12.2	3.5	3.8	2.3	4.0	2.8	4.8	10.9	3.4	2.3	33.1	26.3
3. Bihar	39.4	16.8	5.2	4.0	1.4	1.6	2.8	6.5	2.4	1.2	51.3	39.0
4. Gujarat	4.2	2.6	3.7	3.0	9.8	16.5	10.2	13.6	16.4	1.1	49.2	53.5
5. Haryana**	-	8.4	-	7.2	-	3.4	-	5.4	-	0.5	-	34.9
6. Himachal Pradesh*	-	11.3	-	3.7	-	2.8	-	11.3	-	0.2	-	39.3
7. Jammu & Kashmir	1.6	0.4	0.8	1.8	12.8	24.8	7.2	16.8	7.4	0.6	31.4	49.3
8. Karnataka	53.9	16.6	1.5	6.5	5.7	3.8	5.6	9.4	5.7	1.0	70.0	55.2
9. Kerala	9.2	2.0	2.4	4.4	5.0	3.5	7.8	12.6	30.2	2.1	50.7	35.8
10. Madhya Pradesh	16.9	10.0	15.4	10.3	6.2	6.3	1.4	4.2	1.5	1.1	47.0	42.2
11. Maharashtra	9.0	5.2	2.8	2.8	1.1	5.2	5.4	10.7	2.7	1.1	45.1	54.3
12. Orissa	6.9	10.6	9.6	5.9	0.6	0.8	0.4	4.4	1.8	1.2	25.6	32.0
13. Punjab**	21.6	5.5	9.9	4.5	2.5	17.4	11.0	14.2	8.1	2.0	55.8	58.1
14. Rajasthan	20.3	15.1	23.8	12.3	11.6	19.2	4.6	10.1	6.3	3.4	58.6	57.5
15. Tamil Nadu	53.5	22.8	5.2	11.2	1.8	3.1	2.8	12.8	3.2	1.9	64.3	60.5
16. Uttar Pradesh	21.6	10.5	9.3	9.1	2.2	2.4	5.3	7.1	3.6	1.4	43.6	38.1
17. West Bengal	16.4	5.9	2.5	6.9	3.5	2.9	6.5	11.2	5.5	0.8	46.1	39.4
18. All India	25.0	11.5	7.8	6.8	4.2	5.2	4.6	8.8	5.1	1.5	49.6	44.4

Note: * Data not available for 1961.
** Figures shown against Punjab for 1961 are inclusive of Haryana.

Source: Statistical Tables on Household Debt and Investment, All India Debt and Investment Survey, 1971–72, Reserve Bank of India, Bombay.

Table 3.17: Share of cash debt against different purposes to total cash debt of cultivators-Statewise (as on June 30)

(Percentage)

States	*Repayment of debt*		*Financial investment expenditure*		*Others*		*More than one purpose*		*Unspecified*		*Total*	
	1962	*1971*	*1962*	*1971*	*1962*	*1971*	*1962*	*1971*	*1962*	*1971*	*1962*	*1971*
(1)	*(2)*	*(3)*	*(4)*	*(5)*	*(6)*	*(7)*	*(8)*	*(9)*	*(10)*	*(11)*	*(12)*	*(13)*
1. Andhra Pradesh	7.0	2.1	0.3	1.2	0.4	5.1	6.8	0.4	0.2	0.2	100.0	100.0
2. Assam	1.7	1.2	0.1	1.4	1.0	10.8	3.8	0.6	0.1	0.1	100.0	100.0
3. Bihar	5.5	3.5	Neg.	0.7	Neg.	14.8	1.9	0.2	0.1	0.2	100.0	100.0
4. Gujarat	1.4	0.6	Neg.	Neg.	–	1.0	0.2	0.1	0.1	0.7	100.0	100.0
5. Haryana*	–	1.2	–	0.1	–	4.9	–	0.9	–	–	–	100.0
6. Himachal Pradesh	N.A.	–	N.A.	–	N.A.	8.0	N.A.	–	N.A.	Neg.	N.A.	100.0
7. Jammu & Kashmir	0.2	0.1	–	1.0	–	14.4	0.7	–	Neg.	0.1	100.0	100.0
8. Karnataka	6.7	0.9	0.4	0.9	Neg.	2.9	0.9	0.5	0.9	0.4	100.0	100.0
9. Kerala	13.4	5.6	0.7	5.3	–	7.8	2.7	Neg.	0.5	2.7	100.0	100.0
10. Madhya Pradesh	4.2	1.2	0.1	0.3	–	1.9	1.5	0.8	0.3	0.1	100.0	100.0
11. Maharashtra	0.9	0.5	0.2	0.3	–	1.6	1.2	Neg.	–	0.1	100.0	100.0
12. Orissa	2.1	1.1	0.4	2.5	Neg.	11.4	3.0	0.2	0.4	Neg.	100.0	100.0
13. Punjab*	4.3	1.7	Neg.	0.3	0.5	3.5	2.2	–	1.5	–	100.0	100.0
14. Rajasthan	2.9	1.5	0.3	0.1	0.1	5.3	2.3	0.2	1.6	0.3	100.0	100.0
15. Tamil Nadu	8.2	1.8	0.3	0.3	–	2.0	6.4	0.4	–	0.3	100.0	100.0
16. Uttar Pradesh	4.9	1.4	Neg.	0.6	0.4	6.5	3.0	0.1	0.5	0.2	100.0	100.0
17. West Bengal	2.6	0.9	0.1	0.1	–	4.3	0.2	0.5	–	0.3	100.0	100.0
18. All India	5.0	1.5	0.2	0.7	0.2	4.7	3.0	0.3	0.5	0.3	100.0	100.0

Note: * Figures shown against Punjab for 1962 are inclusive of Haryana.
N.A. = Not available. Neg. = Negligible. Note: Totals may not add up due to rounding.

(Contd.)

Table 3.17: *(Contd.)*

(Percentage)

States	*Capital expenditure on farm business*		*Current expenditure on farm business*		*Capital expenditure on non–farm business*		*Current expenditure on non–farm business*		*Household expenditure*		*Expenditure on litigation*	
	1962	1971	1962	1971	1962	1971	1962	1971	1962	1971	1962	1971
(1)	(2)	(3)	(4)	(5)	(6)	(7)	(8)	(9)	(10)	(11)	(12)	(13)
1. Andhra Pradesh	32.0	31.7	9.4	18.0	0.9	2.8	1.6	0.9	40.6	37.2	0.8	0.4
2. Assam	27.3	27.7	12.9	12.2	1.7	12.8	1.3	0.7	47.0	29.5	3.1	3.0
3. Bihar	11.1	16.5	4.3	5.3	1.2	1.7	1.4	0.3	70.9	54.5	3.7	2.3
4. Gujarat	26.1	42.5	19.3	20.4	0.7	1.9	0.5	0.5	51.4	32.2	0.2	0.1
5. Haryana*	–	54.3	–	11.1	–	3.2	–	–	–	23.9	–	0.4
6. Himachal Pradesh	N.A.	20.7	N.A.	5.7	N.A.	9.6	N.A.	1.5	N.A.	50.7	N.A.	3.8
7. Jammu & Kashmir	10.1	8.9	0.6	3.4	0.5	14.9	3.1	3.4	81.1	53.5	3.7	0.3
8. Karnataka	30.9	34.9	11.0	16.1	0.4	1.6	1.6	0.8	46.0	40.8	1.2	0.2
9. Kerala	20.9	14.6	5.9	12.1	1.6	10.1	6.1	7.5	47.6	33.9	0.6	0.5
10. Madhya Pradesh	30.9	33.4	9.8	18.8	0.4	3.1	3.0	0.8	48.9	39.3	0.8	0.3
11. Maharashtra	29.8	45.1	33.4	31.6	6.0	2.7	1.5	1.2	26.8	16.9	0.3	0.1
12. Orissa	19.1	22.1	3.0	6.4	2.2	5.5	6.2	2.0	62.6	47.2	1.0	1.6
13. Punjab*	25.0	48.6	3.0	12.0	1.1	2.6	1.2	0.2	57.4	29.7	3.9	1.4
14. Rajasthan	25.6	23.2	3.9	5.2	1.0	1.7	2.8	1.9	59.1	59.2	0.4	1.4
15. Tamil Nadu	39.0	44.9	10.3	15.6	2.0	3.5	0.8	1.0	31.8	29.6	1.2	0.6
16. Uttar Pradesh	24.2	34.8	4.5	7.9	1.0	2.6	3.4	0.9	53.9	43.9	4.1	1.1
17. West Bengal	12.5	28.5	15.5	15.5	1.5	3.1	4.6	1.9	61.1	44.9	2.1	Neg.
18. All India	26.8	34.7	9.8	15.0	1.4	3.2	2.1	1.1	49.2	37.8	1.8	0.7

Note: * Figures shown against Punjab for 1962 are inclusive of Haryana.
N.A. = Not available. Neg. = Negligible.

Source: Statistical Tables on Household Debt & Investment, All India Debt and Investment Survey, 1971–72, Reserve Bank of India, Bombay.

Table 3.18: Proportion of cultivator households reporting cash debt for different purposes according to asset groups—All India (As on 30.6.1971)

(Percentage)

Purpose	Asset group (Rs.)										
	0–500	500–1000	1000–2500	2500–5000	5000–10000	10000–15000	15000–20000	20000–30000	30000–50000	50000–100000	100000 & above	Total
(1)	(2)	(3)	(4)	(5)	(6)	(7)	(8)	(9)	(10)	(11)	(12)	(13)
1. Capital expenditure on farm business	2.4	2.9	5.1	7.6	10.3	12.4	13.6	17.4	19.6	21.8	24.8	11.1
2. Current expenditure on farm business	2.6	3.0	4.6	6.3	8.3	10.1	12.2	12.1	14.0	15.0	15.6	8.7
3. Capital expenditure on non–farm business	0.9	0.9	0.6	0.9	1.0	1.3	1.0	0.9	1.1	1.5	1.5	1.0
4. Current expenditure on non–farm business	0.3	0.6	0.5	0.5	0.5	0.6	0.5	0.6	0.5	0.6	0.6	0.5
5. Household expenditure	29.0	29.3	30.9	29.6	27.3	25.6	23.1	22.6	19.4	17.6	13.1	26.3
6. Expenditure on litigation	0.3	0.2	0.3	0.1	0.3	0.3	0.4	0.4	0.4	0.4	0.6	0.3
7. Repayment of debt	0.4	0.4	0.7	0.8	0.8	0.7	1.1	0.9	0.3	0.7	1.2	0.3
8. Financial investment expenditure	0.2	0.2	0.2	0.3	0.3	0.4	0.2	0.5	0.2	0.4	0.3	0.3
9. Others	1.9	2.9	2.0	2.6	2.6	2.3	2.5	2.2	2.3	2.6	2.4	2.4
10. More than one purpose	–	–	0.1	0.1	0.1	0.1	0.1	0.1	0.2	0.1	0.4	0.1
11. Unspecified	Neg.	0.1	0.1	0.2	0.1	0.1	0.2	0.1	0.2	0.3	0.3	0.1
Total	35.4	38.2	41.3	43.3	44.6	46.1	45.6	47.5	47.7	47.3	47.4	44.4

Note: Neg. = Negligible.

Source: Statistical Tables on Household Debt & Investment, All India Debt and Investment Survey, 1971–72, Reserve Bank of India, Bombay.

commercial banks, agriculture was considered the important priority sector and the making of the provision for agricultural credit as an important instrument for development of agriculture was not seriously thought of. As a result, cultivators had to depend entirely on the mercy of the landlords, money-lenders and various kinds of commission agents even at the risk of going under permanent debt bondage of the usurious private moneylenders and designing landlords. With the change of government credit policy for rural areas and agriculture, the situation started taking a new direction. Since the nationalisation of Banks in 1969, and government's direct intervention through different schemes in accelerating the credit flow to the rural areas, the source pattern of rural credit had undergone a change and the dominance of the sources of non-institutional credit started reducing and institutional credit began to be recognised as an important instrument for effecting progressive change. However, the cultivator households who could not satisfy the conditionalities of the commercial or co-operative banking institutions, had to fall back upon the non-institutional private moneylenders or to depend solely on their meagre means. These section of the cultivator households had no alternative but to carry on their farm business following the traditional pattern and for augmenting their farm production they took resort to intensive use of land, intensive use of household or hired labour and spare use of modern inputs to the extent their means permitted given, of course, the availability of water for cultivation. In the farms, where irrigation water was also scarce, even such marginal improvement could not be attempted and cultivation remained tied to the age-old land-bullock-labour technology depending exclusively on rain water. To appraise the nature of the impact of the government credit policy pursued, since sixties, let us look into the data given in Tables 3.14 through 3.18.

Two broad findings from the data are given as under:

1. Although a substantial portion of the credit is used to meet the household consumption needs of the cultivator households, a bulk allocation is made for

capital expenditure in farm business. Allocation for current expenditure in farm business, for paying off old debts, for other non-farm business etc., follows in descending order of importance. It might also be seen that compared to the priorities assigned for allocation to the different items of expenditure in 1961-62, the priority for allocation changed in 1971-72 when higher priority, in most of the states, was found to be assigned to capital expenditure in farm business and the lower to the household consumption needs, only negligible proportions having been allocated for other items.

2. Regarding allocation of credit to different items of expenditure two different patterns emerged, one for the so-called Group I states and the other for the Group II states. In the former group of states about 50 per cent or in the case of a few states belonging to the group more than 50 per cent of the total amount of credit obtained in any year (particularly in 1971-72 compared to 1961-62) was found to be allocated for productive purposes with a substantial proportion being allocated for capital expenditure in farm business and the remaining bulk being allocated for household consumption. In the Group II states, on the other hand, although the proportion allocated for productive expenditure which included capital expenditure in farm business, remained sizeable, the proportion allocated for household consumption got the highest priority.
3. The significance of non-institutional private money-lenders which remained at a commanding position with respect to supply of credit to the rural areas till 1951-52 having controlled about 70 per cent of the rural credit came down to 31 per cent in 1971-72, whereas during the same period, government, commercial banks and co-operatives as the operating institutional credit agencies in rural areas, emerged as growing agencies for rural credit management as their respective share in total rural credit, compared to their

corresponding share in 1951-52, indicated manifold increase in 1971-72. The emergence of co-operative as the leading credit agency among them, however, was observed to be distinctly clear. The situation thus indicated a signal of at least a partial slackening of the grip of rural money-lenders over the farming community and a progressive extension of benefit handed out by the government credit policy adopted since sixties (see Table 3.15). The data on state-wise breakdown of rural credit by credit agencies (see Table 3.16) indicated almost a similar pattern in most of the major states of the country. But, among the three institutional credit agencies, the significant role of co-operative could be noticed, particularly for Gujarat, Maharashtra, Karnataka, Punjab, Haryana, Tamil Nadu etc., which earlier in this chapter had been categorised as Group I states, although in Bihar, Orissa, Uttar Pradesh, Madhya Pradesh and Kerala also their growing importance should not escape notice. In spite of the fact that proportionate share of credit supply to rural areas directly by the government and commercial banks increased over the two decades, their proportion to total credit, however remained still too small and also the co-operatives failed to function effectively in all the states. Thus the assistance rendered by institutional credit to the needy farmers in rural areas remained in a sense discriminatory as it could not reach uniformly to the different states.

Our main contention of the diminishing influence of non-institutional agencies in the rural credit market and increasing preference of the farming community for institutional agencies particularly the co-operatives, both in the country as a whole and also in different states, found ample corroboration in the data given in Table 3.16. In this Table, the changed pattern of preference, over a decade (between 1961-62 and 1971-72), for credit agencies has been shown. It is clearly seen that as source of credit, the cultivator households express increasing preference for co-operatives, commercial banks and government and their disenchantment towards private non-institutional agencies, grow consequentially. It should, however, be noted from the same set of data that non-institutional agencies continued to exercise their grip over the rural credit market in quite a large number of states which were categorised as Group II and where, because of the lower per household average size of operational holding and the use of traditional type of capital structure in the farm business, the cultivator households perhaps was considered less credit worthy as the value of the asset-holding they own is generally too low to obtain institutional credit. But agricultural and landlord moneylenders, most likely because of their long standing economic liaison with the cultivator households and of their social dominance over the local population, could venture to take risk to advance credit to those cultivator households who were otherwise considered non-credit worthy by the institutional agencies.

4

Nature of Capital Formation in Agricultural Economy

Results of the Case Study in West Bengal

The short description of the pattern of capital formation in Indian agriculture presented in chapter three shows the direction of the change of capital structure in Indian agriculture over a little more than three decades at the all-India and state level. The contemporary picture of the nature of capital formation in rural farm business at the level of district and village in the state of West Bengal has been studied against this backgrounds. This was planned to bring within the forms of study the situation of the capital formation obtaining at the three different levels in the country as a whole, the state and the lowest level of villages in a state so that on the dynamics of the transformation of capital structure in agriculture, some meaningful conclusions could be formulated on this basis.

In this chapter, the results of the village level case study, conducted as an integral part of this research scheme, in the two districts of West Bengal, the districts of Bardhaman and South 24-Paraganas, are presented. In view of the inter-state variation of the characteristics of capital formation, which is well-known, it would have been an ideal exercise to conduct similar case studies in a few villages in each of major states of the country. But conduct of case studies to cover such a wide area of the country, being too expensive a venture, became difficult to be fitted in, within this low financed research scheme. But since the conditions of agriculture in West Bengal, at least in so far as the nature of capital structure is concerned, can well be compared with similar conditions prevailing in a large number of so-called less developed or developing states; the results of this case study can well be considered as reflecting the nature of change in fixed capital structure in rural farm business for at least the similar areas of the country, where agriculture still remains in a developing stage.

In regard to the modernisation of agriculture, West Bengal, as we know, belongs to the less advanced group of states. But here also there are relatively advanced and relatively backward areas. For the case study, therefore, we have purposively selected one district considered as advanced and the other which is known as relatively backward from the point of view of agricultural development. The district of Bardhaman belongs to the advanced category, while the district of South 24-Paraganas belongs to the backward category. The overall condition in agricultural development measured in terms of agricultural production, the state of irrigation and lastly, the convenience of the field inquiry were the three broad criteria on the basis of which the two districts for the case study were selected. Six villages within each district were selected purposively. Out of the six villages selected from each district, three come from areas located nearer to town and the other three from areas remote from the town. This was done anticipating that the proximity and remoteness of the selected villages from the town or the market area would have corresponding favourable or adverse effect on the growth and development of the farm business and also on the behaviour pattern of the cultivator households, particularly in taking crucial decisions on relevant matters related to the development of the farm business. Having selected both the districts and the villages in this manner, the sample households in which the field survey was conducted were chosen at random from a complete list of households made in each of the selected villages hamlets in the case of big village, through house listing operation. The household survey in two villages, was carried out by trained investigators, through house to house interview of the household members or the head of households whichever was found to be convenient for eliciting better and reliable information. Altogether 75 households, from each of the two categories of villages in each of two selected districts, were sampled for the conduct of the household survey. 150 households from each of two districts were selected for the detailed household survey. Two different forms were designed for the collection of information in the villages and households one for listing of households in the village or hamlet for collection of information required for selection of households and the other for the collection of detailed information from each of the sampled households.

Having taken into account the problem of re-call of information with reference to a long period in the past and the complicated nature of data on capital formation and indebtedness proposed to be collected form the households, a very simple schedule has been designed. Since the data would be collected through a single visit of the households, emphasis was laid on only those items of data which were considered feasible for collection with ease avoiding the hazard of informants fatigue. The household schedule was designed to collect following items of information:

1. Household's social and economic characteristics, such as household occupation, household size, household land owned and possessed etc.
2. Household asset-holding including capital assets in use in household farm and non-farm business as on the date of survey.
3. Household consumption expenditure with reference to one week for ordinary consumer items and one year for durable or semi-durable consumer goods.
4. Capital expenditure made during the year ending on the date of survey.
5. Saving habit of households.
6. Disbursement of saving.
7. Indebtedness of households.

The results of the survey are presented in the following section. While presenting the results, some relevant results of the all-India debt and investment survey conducted in 1981-82 relating to West Bengal have also been presented side-by-side to see how the results of the case study conform to, or, deviate from the results of the all-India survey. If wide divergence is observed we may try to explore the plausible reason for that.

Before we discuss the results of the case study, it will be quite in order to mention about a few relevant economic characteristics relating to rural areas and agriculture for the two districts—Bardhaman and South 24-Paraganas. The district of Bardhaman is known to be very rich in agricultural production and considered the granary of West Bengal, although the Asansol, Durgapur, Raniganj belt of the districts is industrially developed and essentially urban. Also the district is endowed with sufficiently developed road and transport network which connects the rural areas with the markets and urban centres. The district of South 24-Paraganas, on the other hand, is relatively more backward in agriculture compared to Bardhaman and predominantly rural. In a portion of the district, though, there are important centres of manufacturing industries spread over along the eastern bank of Hooghly river.

Some salient economic characteristics considered relevant and important for agriculture for the two districts have been compiled from the 1981 Census District Handbook and are shown in Table 4.1.

Table 4.1: A few important economic characteristics of the two districts

Sl. No.	*Economic characteristics*	*Bardhaman*	*South 24-Paraganas*
(1)	*(2)*	*(3)*	*(4)*
1.	Total population according to 1981	48.35 lakhs	49.56 lakhs
2.	P.C. of rural population	78.61	77.16
3.	Decadal growth (1971–1981)	23.47	–
4.	P.C. of cultivated land to total land area	82.17	75.18
5.	P.C. of land irrigated to total land cultivated	59.35	5.55
6.	P.C. of total workers	30.61	26.61
7.	P.C. of agricultural labourers	23.61	25.97

Similar information, for only the eight selected police station areas in the two districts from which the villages have been sampled, are given in Table 4.2. These economic parameters may be useful for having a proper feel about the prevailing conditions of agriculture in the adjoining areas around the villages selected for the case study.

The data presented in Table 4.2 clearly show that the two areas selected for the case study in the two districts of West Bengal are predominantly rural and the land use pattern of the area as per 1981 Census enumeration is almost constrained to be dependent mainly on agriculture and allied activities although as a deterrent factor the weak irrigation facilities available in South 24-Paraganas cannot be overlooked.

The other relevant economic feature of the area (not shown in this Table) which determine the character of agricultural activities in the area are:

(i) Predominance of self-employment in cultivation and allied activities,
(ii) Proportion of wage-labour compared to household labour rather low,
(iii) Low work participation rate of population,
(iv) Very low (20 to 30 per cent of the rural population), work participation rate of women.

All these provides at least some evidence, though not a conclusive evidence, of agriculture in the area being considered more as an important subsistence sector by the households rather than a sector for a market economy.

From the results of the household survey conducted in the area, in the selected households presented below, we shall examine to what extent the general observation made about the area tally with the specific situation obtaining in a much smaller area brought under the coverage of the survey.

Table 4.2: A few important economic characteristics of the eight selected police stations

Economic characteristics	*District Bardhaman*				*District South 24–Paraganas*			
	Police Station				*Police Station*			
	Bardhaman	*Katwa*	*Galsi*	*Bhatar*	*Bishnupur*	*Jaynagar*	*Bhangar*	*Mograhat*
(1)	(2)	(3)	(4)	(5)	(6)	(7)	(8)	(9)
1. Total population (1981 Census)	351413	256372	173592	179233	287811	254478	248071	218136
2. P.C. of rural population	–	–	–	–	95.75	93.58	100.0	100.0
3. P.C. of cultivated land to total land	80.48	82.61	81.25	83.03	72.00	83.14	71.95	79.12
4. P.C. of land irrigated to total land	78.81	58.00	81.08	87.10	7.61	6.91	11.91	–
5. P.C. of total worker to total population	29.06	28.02	32.72	30.18	26.20	25.68	27.75	25.08
6. P.C. of agricultural labourer to total worker	30.15	29.18	48.47	47.29	31.17	34.46	30.34	34.23

Occupational Pattern of Households

The results of the household survey showing distribution of households by their principal occupation is given in Table 4.3. Occupational scenario of the villages studied, however, is observed to be somewhat different from that of the broader police station area. This difference is quite possible as villages from the police station areas have been purposively selected and even though the households from the selected villages have been chosen at random, the agricultural labour households have been purposefully omitted from the last stage selection of households in view of the fact that for the data on capital formation or capital expenditure, the contribution of agricultural labour households will be negligible.

The results of the households survey have revealed that although agriculture and allied activities remains the principal economic activity of the largest proportion of the total number of households surveyed both in villages nearer to and remote from town. For both the districts selected for the case study, the predominance of agriculture and allied activities as has been observed in the wider police station areas has not been visible among the households surveyed. In both the districts, among households belonging to both the types of villages chosen, significant presence of other activities related to manufacture, trade and transport has been observed. Of course, in the villages remote from town, agriculture and allied activities occupy a relatively higher position in order of importance in the sense of that being the principal occupation of proportionately larger number of households than their corresponding proportion in villages nearer to town.

This is an understandable situation as the proximity from the urban area provides these villages added advantage of utilising the urban infrastructural facilities for procurement of necessary raw materials and for sale of products or merchandise or for getting larger number of transportation trips etc. But the presence of large number of non-agricultural economic units even in villages remote from town in South 24-Paraganas is difficult to explain. Quite likely, agriculture not being very lucrative in the area, the proximity of the district from the City of Calcutta itself, and the presence of wide network of all weather roads connecting the village with Calcutta encouraged the growth of viable non-agricultural productive units even in the remote villages of the district even though more than 50 per cent of the households in these villages have agriculture and allied activities as principal occupation. Significant growth of infrastructural facilities over the last two decades in and around the rural areas of both the districts has opened up alternative avenues of employment and income in these non-agricultural pursuits and instead of depending solely on agriculture which is beset with various limiting factors of growth, they try their luck in these prospective growth sectors.

Another interesting feature of the occupational pattern of the area covered by the households is the intertwining relationship between the principal and the main secondary occupation of the households. This is evidenced by the data on distribution of households by their principal and secondary occupations shown in Table 4.4. It is observed that about 60-70 per cent of the total number of households surveyed, the percentage proportion varying within this range between the types of villages chosen in two districts, have more than one household occupations but each one of them has some link, strong or weak, with agriculture and only about 30-40 per cent of the households reported to have only one household occupation—agriculture or non-agricultural as the case may be.

It may also be noted from the Table that, especially in the case of villages remote from town, such intertwining relationship between agriculture and non-agricultural units pursued either as principal or secondary household occupation is very strong while in the other set of villages such relationship is rather weak. The pattern of the kind of inter-relationship reflected in the data, speak of an important fact of agricultural economy that prevails in large number of villages placed in the similar situation as obtains in the villages of the two districts chosen. It will be quite in order to state that for a large number of rural households in the types of villages chosen, either

Table 4.3: Percentage distribution of households by principal occupation by type of villages and by districts

Principal sector of household economic activity	*Percentage of households*					
	Bardhaman			*South 24–Paraganas*		
	Villages nearer to town	*Villages remote from town*	*All villages*	*Villages nearer to town*	*Villages remote from town*	*All villages*
(1)	(2)	(3)	(4)	(5)	(6)	(7)
1. Cultivation	27.9	40.0	34.1	32.1	48.0	40.0
2. Other allied activities (animal husbandry, poultry, fishing, forestry, horticulture etc.)	9.3	–	4.7	1.3	2.7	2.0
3. Manufacturing including industrial services, craftsman and industrial worker	18.7	17.3	17.9	28.0	18.7	23.4
4. Trading (wholesale and retail)	18.7	20.0	19.3	16.0	16.0	16.0
5. Construction including construction worker—skilled and unskilled	4.0	–	2.0	4.0	–	2.0
6. Transport operation including manually operated transport	14.7	14.7	14.7	13.3	6.7	10.0
7. Public services including health and other personal services	6.7	8.0	7.3	5.3	7.9	6.6
Total	100.0	100.0	100.0	100.0	100.0	100.0

Table 4.4: Percentage distribution of households under each household principal occupation category by household secondary occupation category and village types separately for the districts

Principal household occupation category	Villages nearer to town: Secondary household occupation category						Villages remote from town: Secondary household occupation category						All villages: Secondary household occupation category					
	Agriculture and allied activities	*Manufacturing*	*Trade*	*Transport*	*Others*	*Nil*	*Agriculture and allied activities*	*Manufacturing*	*Trade*	*Transport*	*Others*	*Nil*	*Agriculture and allied activities*	*Manufacturing*	*Trade*	*Transport*	*Others*	*Nil*
(1)	(2)	(3)	(4)	(5)	(6)	(7)	(8)	(9)	(10)	(11)	(12)	(13)	(14)	(15)	(16)	(17)	(18)	(19)
District: Bardhaman																		
1. Agriculture and allied activities	53.6	17.9	10.7	–	7.1	10.7	63.4	3.3	13.3	–	13.3	6.7	58.6	10.4	12.1	–	10.2	8.6
2. Manufacturing	28.6	7.1	7.1	–	–	57.2	63.6	–	–	–	–	36.4	44.0	4.0	4.0	–	–	48.0
3. Trade	64.3	–	–	–	21.4	14.3	80.0	–	–	–	–	20.0	72.4	–	–	–	10.3	17.3
4. Transport	–	50.0	–	–	–	50.0	100.0	–	–	–	–	–	50.0	25.0	–	–	–	25.0
5. Others	23.3	11.8	–	–	23.5	41.2	58.8	–	5.9	–	11.8	23.5	41.2	5.9	2.9	–	17.6	32.4
All	42.7	12.0	5.3	–	12.0	28.0	66.7	1.3	6.7	–	8.0	17.3	54.7	6.7	6.0	–	10.0	22.6
District: South 24-Paraganas																		
1. Agriculture and allied activities	64.0	4.0	4.0	–	20.0	8.0	47.4	5.3	13.2	–	18.4	15.7	54.0	4.8	9.5	–	19.0	12.7
2. Manufacturing	42.9	–	–	–	4.8	52.3	71.4	–	–	–	21.4	7.2	54.3	–	–	–	11.4	34.3
3. Trade	58.3	–	–	–	–	41.7	91.7	–	–	–	–	8.3	75.0	–	–	–	–	25.0
4. Transport	–	–	–	–	–	100.0	100.0	–	–	–	–	–	40.0	–	–	–	–	60.0
5. Others	35.7	7.1	–	–	7.2	50.0	88.9	–	–	–	–	11.1	56.5	4.4	–	–	4.3	34.8
All	49.2	2.7	1.3	–	9.3	37.4	65.3	2.7	6.7	–	13.3	12.0	57.3	2.7	4.0	–	11.3	24.7

agriculture or non-agricultural, household unit is not in a position to stand on their own legs and require, one or more, than one supporting units to meet the required needs of household.

Scale of Non-agricultural Units in Survey Villages

In view of significant presence of non-agricultural productive units in the villages studied we should be aware about the scale of such units with a view to finding out whether their existence in the village economy are only nominal or really worthwhile. In the survey, the data on the amount of annual turnover of non-agricultural units were collected. Even presuming that the likely tendency among the reporting households would be to underquote the value of annual turnover, the relative position of the household non-agricultural units between themselves would not, however, be disturbed unduly since by the phenomenon of underquoting of the value will affect all household units more or less uniformly and it will be in the same direction. It may be seen from Table 4.5 given below that both in Bardhaman and South 24-Paraganas, irrespective of whether the villages are located nearer to or remote from town, about 60-70 per cent of the total number of units are small in the sense that the annual value of turnover reported by them occur in the range Rs. 10,000-20,000. There are larger units with annual value of turnover ranging between Rs. 50,000-1,00,000 between Rs. 1,00,000-2,00,000 and between Rs. 2,00,000 and above, but their number is proportionately very small and their presence in villages nearer to town is proportionately higher than those in villages remote from town.

Activity Pattern of Population

The distribution of population of the sample households in the surveyed villages by their activity pattern as obtained in the reference week is shown in Table 4.6. It may be observed that in the survey villages, the reported overall work-participation rate of population for both the districts shown in the Table is only about 30 per cent, with varying rate of 31-33 per cent for households selected from South 24-Paraganas and 29-31 per cent for households selected from Bardhaman. It may also be observed that for both the districts, the male and female work-participation rates are in the range of 45-51 per cent and 5-6 per cent respectively. It may be noted that both the overall rate as well as the sex specific rates are quite below the State level rate.

Another important feature of the activity pattern of the population of the sample households to be observed is the preponderance of self-employment and a very low proportion of wage-labour in both the sets of villages surveyed: the observed proportion of wage-labour in the population, though, is higher in villages nearer to town than that in villages remote from town.

Table 4.5: Percentage distribution of households having non-agricultural activities as principal occupation by total turn-over (in Rs.)

Total turn-over group (in Rs.)	*Bardhaman*			*South 24–Paraganas*		
	Villages nearer to town	*Villages remote from town*	*All villages*	*Villages nearer to town*	*Villages remote from town*	*All villages*
(1)	(2)	(3)	(4)	(5)	(6)	(7)
0–3000	6.4	–	3.3	–	–	–
3000–5000	–	–	–	2.0	–	1.1
5000–10000	19.1	26.7	22.8	18.0	13.5	16.1
10000–20000	40.5	48.9	44.6	42.0	22.6	33.3
20000–30000	2.1	6.7	4.3	10.0	8.1	9.2
30000–50000	4.3	–	2.2	4.0	13.5	8.1
50000–100000	6.4	4.4	5.4	8.0	13.5	10.4
100000–200000	10.6	8.9	9.8	12.0	16.3	13.6
200000 & above	10.6	4.4	7.6	4.0	13.6	8.0
All	100.0	100.0	100.0	100.0	100.0	100.0

Size-distribution of Ownership Holding

In presenting the profile of the nature and characteristics of capital formation in agriculture in chapter three, it has been observed that the average size of operational holding in a group

Table 4.6: Percentage of households by activity and sex.

Base : Each Sex

District : South 24–Paraganas

Activity status	*Sex*		
	Male	*Female*	*All*
(1)	*(2)*	*(3)*	*(4)*
(i) Villages nearer to town			
1. Employer	2.5	–	1.4
2. Employee	2.9	0.4	1.7
3. Self-employed	45.8	5.9	27.5
4. Sub-total : workforce	51.2	6.3	30.6
5. Unemployed	2.5	0.4	1.5
6. House workers	0.3	42.4	19.6
7. Student	20.8	17.1	19.1
8. Too young to work, too old, infirm or disabled, pensioners, rentiers etc.	25.2	33.8	29.2
9. Sub-total : out of labour force	46.3	93.3	67.9
10. All	100.0	100.0	100.0
(ii) Villages remote from town			
1. Employer	2.2	–	1.2
2. Employee	3.4	–	1.9
3. Self-employed	41.8	4.2	24.9
4. Sub-total : workforce	47.4	4.2	28.0
5. Unemployed	2.1	–	1.2
6. House workers	1.5	49.0	22.9
7. Student	24.8	20.9	23.0
8. Too young to work, too old, infirm or disabled, pensioners, rentiers etc.	24.2	25.9	24.9
9. Sub-total : out of labour force	50.5	95.8	70.8
10. All	100.0	100.0	100.0
(iii) All villages			
1. Employer	2.3	–	1.3
2. Employee	3.1	0.2	1.8
3. Self-employed	43.8	5.1	26.2
4. Sub-total : workforce	49.2	5.3	29.3
5. Unemployed	2.3	0.2	1.4
6. House workers	0.9	45.6	21.2
7. Student	22.8	19.0	21.1
8. Too young to work, too old, infirm or disabled, pensioners, rentiers etc.	24.8	29.9	27.0
9. Sub-total : out of labour force	48.5	94.5	69.3
10. All	100.0	100.0	100.0

(Contd.)

Table 4.6: (*Contd.*)

Base : Each Sex

District : Bardhaman			
Activity status	*Sex*		
	Male	*Female*	*All*
(1)	(2)	(3)	(4)
(i) Villages nearer to town			
1. Employer	–	–	–
2. Employee	8.8	1.3	5.4
3. Self-employed	44.9	5.7	27.1
4. Sub-total : workforce	53.7	7.0	32.5
5. Unemployed	2.9	0.9	2.0
6. House workers	0.4	52.9	24.3
7. Student	22.8	22.9	22.8
8. Too young to work, too old, infirm or disabled, pensioners, rentiers etc.	20.2	16.3	18.4
9. Sub-total : out of labour force	43.4	92.1	65.5
10. All	100.0	100.0	100.0
(ii) Villages remote from town			
1. Employer	–	–	–
2. Employee	4.7	2.7	3.8
3. Self-employed	50.4	0.8	26.3
4. Sub-total : workforce	55.1	3.5	30.1
5. Unemployed	1.5	–	0.3
6. House workers	–	51.5	25.0
7. Student	24.3	21.7	23.3
8. Too young to work, too old, infirm or disabled, pensioners, rentiers etc.	18.6	23.3	20.3
9. Sub-total : out of labour force	43.4	96.5	69.1
10. All	100.0	100.0	100.0
(iii) All villages			
1. Employer	–	–	–
2. Employee	6.3	2.1	4.6
3. Self-employed	47.6	3.1	26.6
4. Sub-total : workforce	54.4	5.2	31.2
5. Unemployed	2.2	0.4	1.4
6. House workers	0.2	52.1	24.6
7. Student	23.3	22.3	23.1
8. Too young to work, too old, infirm or disabled, pensioners, rentiers etc.	19.4	20.0	19.7
9. Sub-total : out of labour force	43.4	94.4	67.4
10. All	100.0	100.0	100.0

of states in India, which includes West Bengal, is low compared to the corresponding average size in the other state group. In Table 4.7, the cumulative percentage of total land owned by sample households in the case study villages by the size-class of household land ownership holding is presented along with the similar cumulative distribution for All-India and State of West Bengal available from the results of NSS 37th round survey on land-holding. It is observed from the data shown in Table 4.7 that situation in regard to the size of ownership holding of the households in the considered villages is far worse compared even to the ownership-holding size distribution shown for rural West Bengal. While according to the NSS survey the percentage of total land holding having the size 1 acre or less is only 9.42 per cent in the case of rural West Bengal, the corresponding percentage for the households in the case study villages in Bardhaman is 50 and in South 24-Paraganas is 48. Again, while the percentage of total land-holding having the size 2.49 acres and less is 30.33 per cent in rural West Bengal as per NSS 37th round survey, the corresponding percentage of total holding in the households sampled from case study villages in Bardhaman and South 24-Paraganas has been reported to be 67 and 62 per cent respectively. It is clear that the size of ownership holding of the type of households chosen for the case study, though they have been chosen in a random manner, is unusually small. Since both the districts and villages chosen for the case study were purposively chosen, such wide divergence between the results of a properly organised random survey of the NSS type and the results emanating from a survey conducted in a small number of randomly selected households from only a few villages in only 2 districts of West Bengal, both being selected purposively to suit the limit of cost and time of the case study could not be improbable. So, even though strict comparison is not possible between two sets of data, the results of the case study, nevertheless, reflect the typical condition of agricultural economy prevailing in those rural areas where the case study has been conducted. Against the background of such typical condition of the selected villages, one has to examine the nature and characteristics of capital formation relating to which the data have also been collected in the case study.

Table 4.7: Cumulative percentage distribution of households by size class of household ownership holding

Size class of household ownership holding (acres)	All–India (rural) (NSS 37th round) cumulative percentage of land owned	West Bengal (NSS 37th round) cumulative percentage of land owned	Case study results of cumulative percentage of land owned					
			Bardhaman			South 24–Paraganas		
			Villages nearer to town	Villages remote from town	All villages	Villages nearer to town	Villages remote from town	All villages
(1)	(2)	(3)	(4)	(5)	(6)	(7)	(8)	(9)
1. 0.00	–	–	6.7	5.3	6.0	4.0	–	2.0
2. Upto 0.49	0.90	3.47	56.0	34.7	48.3	53.3	24.0	38.7
3. Upto 0.99	2.75	9.42	58.7	42.7	50.6	61.3	34.7	48.0
4. Upto 2.49	12.22	30.33	77.3	57.4	67.3	72.0	52.0	62.0
5. Upto 4.99	28.71	59.10	89.3	60.7	78.0	96.0	78.7	87.3
6. Upto 7.49	42.55	67.90	96.0	82.7	89.3	98.7	88.0	93.3
7. Upto 9.99	52.09	86.33	96.00	88.0	92.0	100.00	92.0	96.0
8. Upto 14.99	66.73	95.79	100.00	98.7	99.3	100.00	98.7	99.3
9. Upto 19.99	75.55	97.74	100.00	98.7	99.3	100.00	100.00	100.00
10. All sizes	100.00	100.00	100.00	100.00	100.00	100.00	100.00	100.00

Consumption Pattern of Households

Data on household consumption expenditure by various items of consumption and the value of household asset-holding which include both capital assets and consumer durables possessed as on the date of survey have been collected in the household survey conducted in the case study villages from each household surveyed. In the absence of data on monthly or annual income of household, either level of household consumption or value of household asset-holding may be used as a reliable proxy for household income to roughly indicate the economic disposition of household. In the context of the present study on capital formation in agriculture, such indicators may help assessing both the savings and investment potential of the households. In other words, such data may provide some indirect evidence of households demand capabilities for capital goods needed for households' farm or non-farm business. In Table 4.8 is shown the percentage distribution of total household monthly consumption expenditure by food and non-food items and by types of villages where the survey has been conducted in the selected households.

The pattern of consumption expenditure of household, covered by the field survey as revealed from the data shown in Table 4.8, indicates the households are economically better off compared to the average rural households in West Bengal. The capacity to spend higher proportion of total consumption expenditure on non-food items is generally taken as a broad indicator of economic well-being of a population. It is observed that whereas the NSS data on per household consumer expenditure for rural West Bengal[1] report 29 per cent (71% on food item) of total household consumption expenditure spent on non-food items, the percentage of expenditure on non-food items of the total household expenditure recorded in the field survey households varies from 80 to 85 per cent, the small variation recorded being obviously due to the varying location of the villages from town and the inter-district difference of the pattern of consumption expenditure. Although agriculture is reported to be the principal occupation of the majority of the households covered in the case study and among them the proportion of small and marginal farms is very high, the financial disposition of a more or less easy going type as revealed from the consumption expenditure data cannot be explained unless it is assumed that the income generation from other secondary occupations of the household—it has been observed that 70 per cent of the households have one or more than one secondary occupations besides the principal one—push up the total household income and that enable them to maintain a pattern of consumption expenditure which is better than the pattern maintained by the average rural households in West Bengal.

Table 4.8: Percentage distribution of total household monthly consumption expenditure by food and non-food items and by types of villages

District	*Type of villages*	*Percentage of total consumer expenditure*		
		Food	*Non-food*	*Total*
(1)	*(2)*	*(3)*	*(4)*	*(5)*
1. South	Nearer to town	69.2	30.8	100.0
24–Paraganas	Remote from town	65.0	35.0	100.0
	All	67.3	32.7	100.0
2. Bardhaman	Nearer to town	61.4	38.6	100.0
	Remote from town	58.2	41.8	100.0
	All	59.7	40.3	100.0
3. All villages	Nearer to town	65.6	34.4	100.0
	Remote from town	61.7	38.3	100.0
	All	63.6	36.4	100.0

Asset-holding Pattern of Households

The main contention of our argument made above that despite agriculture not being of a very high standard, the households are relatively better off compared to the average rural households in West Bengal, has been further corroborated by the data on the value of household asset-holding collected in the survey. From the data distribution of households by household asset-holding value group given in Table 4.9. It may be observed in all households, irrespective of their locational distance from Urban Centre, the concentration of households is in the asset-holding groups Rs. 20,000-50,000, Rs. 50,000-1,00,000 and Rs. 1,00,000-5,00,000, the maximum concentration being in the last of the above three groups. The three asset-holding groups together cover more than 70 per cent of the total number of households surveyed in all villages and also in the two districts. It may, of course, be mentioned in this connection that the bulk of this asset-holding is constituted of land, both agricultural and other and the escalation of their value is a continuing process particularly because the areas covered by the survey in both the districts are connected with the respective urban centres by well laid network of all weather and metalled road.

Table 4.9: Percentage distribution of households by household asset holding group (in Rs.)

Household asset-holding group (Rs.)	*Bardhaman*			*South 24-Paraganas*		
	Villages nearer to town	*Villages remote from town*	*All villages*	*Villages nearer to town*	*Villages remote from town*	*All villages*
(1)	*(2)*	*(3)*	*(4)*	*(5)*	*(6)*	*(7)*
Upto 1000	–	–	–	–	–	–
1000–5000	1.3	2.7	2.0	2.7	–	1.3
5000–10000	4.0	4.0	4.0	2.7	1.3	2.0
10000–20000	10.7	5.3	8.0	8.0	5.3	6.7
20000–50000	24.0	21.3	22.7	24.0	16.0	20.0
50000–100000	14.7	18.7	16.7	25.3	17.4	21.3
100000–500000	40.0	38.7	39.3	29.3	52.0	40.7
500000 & above	5.3	9.3	7.3	8.0	8.0	8.0
All households	100.0	100.0	100.0	100.0	100.0	100.0

Pattern of Household Savings and their Disposal by Households

So far we have attempted to ascertain the socio-economic disposition of the households on the basis of the data on demographic and other economic characteristics collected from selected households in the case study villages. Before passing on to the topic of capital expenditure and capital formation which is the main focus of the present study, we consider it relevant to present here an outline of the households' savings potential and the nature of their disposal by households based on the data collected in the case study. The purpose is to see whether the data on household savings and their disposal, though quite scanty are, throw some light on the entrepreneurial behaviour of the households towards developing their household agriculture or non-agricultural activities. In Table 4.10 is given the proportion of saving and non-saving households of the total number of households surveyed.

Table 4.10: The proportion of saving and non-saving households by types of villages and districts

Type of villages by districts	*Percentage of total households*	
	Saving households	*Non-saving households*
(1)	*(2)*	*(3)*
Bardhaman:		
Villages nearer to town	57.3	42.7
Villages remote from town	49.3	50.7
All villages in Bardhaman	53.3	46.7
South 24-Paraganas:		
Villages nearer to town	38.7	61.3
Villages remote from town	46.7	53.3
All villages in 24-Paraganas	42.7	57.3

It may be seen that among the two districts, the overall saving potential of households is higher in Bardhaman compared to that in South 24-Paraganas. In both the districts, whether the contribution towards the generation of savings in villages is more from households having agriculture as the principal occupation or from the remaining households having non-agricultural activities as principal occupation becomes clear from the data shown in Table 4.11. It may be seen that whereas in the case of Bardhaman, the contribution of households with agriculture as principal occupation is decisively higher than that of households with non-agricultural activities as principal occupation, the position in the case of South 24-Paraganas villages is just the other way round though there the role of non-agricultural households as the major source of savings is only marginal over the agricultural households, in so far as their contribution to the generation of total savings in the villages. The ratio of contribution of agricultural to non-agricultural households has been observed to be 70:30 in the Bardhaman villages and 49:51 in the case of South 24-Paraganas. It may be noted also that the villages nearer to town in Bardhaman have reported better saving potential whereas in South 24-Paraganas the villages remote from town have reported better savings potential than the other set of villages in the district. Whether or not the factor of nearness or remoteness of the villages from the urban centre have neutral effect on generation of savings in either agricultural or non-agricultural households cannot be judged on the basis of the scanty data forthcoming from the survey. It may be quite possible that better infrastructural facilities in the form of road communication and transport more than offset the difficulties confronted in view of the remoteness of the villages from any urban centre and thus villages nearer to town cannot derive any significant benefit of the locational advantage. Now, what do the villagers do with their household savings? Do they plough back a major part of the savings to household agriculture or to any non-agricultural household enterprise? The data on the nature of disposal of household savings collected in household survey are shown separately for two districts and within a district separately for the two types of villages and also for agricultural and all households taken together in Table 4.12. It is interesting to find that in both the districts and also in both the types of villages as well as in agricultural and other households, only a small amount of household savings is used for making capital expenditure, such as purchase of land and a still smaller amount is spent for capital expenditure on purchase of implements and tools or for current expenditure on purchase materials etc., for other household enterprise. The major bulk of savings is found to be deposited in banks. Another important finding is that the households in Bardhaman villages siphon out a relatively higher amount in making capital (purchase of land or purchase of implements and tools) and current expenditure (purchase of materials for household enterprises) than these made by households in South 24-Paraganas. Although for different set of villages in Bardhaman, the percentage proportion of household savings deposited in banks varies between 56.5 to 76.2 by the agricultural households and 62.8 to 80 by all households taken together in different types of villages surveyed. The corresponding proportion for South 24-Paraganas are 89.4 to 94.4 for agricultural households and 92.6 to 92.9 for all households taken together. Even if we prefer to attach less importance on the figures of proportion, which may change either way if the total number of sample villages and households are enlarged, but only look at the direction of the pattern of disposal of household saving, the conclusion that naturally follows is that for all the different types of households, irrespective of their nearness or remoteness from urban centres, the dominant tendency of the households is to deposit bulk of the savings in banks instead of putting them to other productive uses. The overriding consideration which actuate them to such a decision, most probably, is the assured return from bank deposit as opposed to uncertain return from the doses of investment in household agriculture or in other non-agricultural activities. The other factor which may have influenced their decision-making is that the amount of deposits in banks may enhance their credit worthiness to the bank thereby brightening the prospect of their obtaining bank credit in future when the credit need of both agricultural and non-agricultural activities they pursue will be acutely felt.

Table 4.11: Percentage distribution of total amount saved by district, type of villages and type of households

Type of villages by districts	*Type of households*	*Total amount saved in (Rs.)*	*Percentage distribution*
(1)	*(2)*	*(3)*	*(4)*
Bardhaman :			
Villages nearer to town	Agricultural households	125140	35.78
	All households	188042	53.77
Villages remote from town	Agricultural households	119850	34.27
	All households	161660	46.23
All villages	Agricultural households	244990	70.05
	All households	349702	100.00
South 24-Paraganas:			
Villages nearer to town	Agricultural households	62600	23.66
	All households	125850	47.55
Villages remote from town	Agricultural households	65750	24.85
	All households	138784	52.44
All villages	Agricultural households	128350	48.51
	All households	264634	100.00

In trying to locate the tangible source of savings generation in rural households, ascertaining the relative position of the three or four important sectors of the household economic activity with respect to the generation of savings in the rural households covered in the survey and the pattern of their disposal is important. The relevant survey data are shown in Tables 4.12 and 4.13. It may be seen from Table 4.13 that households having agriculture and allied activities as principal occupation of the households holds the major share (61%) of the total amount of saving generated the other households trailing far behind. Arranging the different categories of households in descending order of importance from the point of view of their contribution to total savings, the trading households (23.3%), the manufacturing households (8.6%) and the households having services as principal occupation (3.8%) respectively occupies the second, third and the fourth position.

As regards the disposal of savings by the households having different principal occupations, it may be noted, the major bulk of the savings are deposited in banks and only about 23 per cent of total amount of savings generated in agricultural households and about 14 per cent of total savings generated in manufacturing households are put to productive (capital and current expenditure) and other uses. In the case of households having other principal occupations than agriculture and manufacturing, very little or nothing is put to any productive or other uses.

Since agricultural households contributes most to the generation of savings in the villages surveyed, it is only natural to ascertain from which section of the agricultural households these savings come and also how they dispose of their savings. The survey data shown in Table 4.14 throw some light on this query. It may be observed that marginal and small farming households, i.e. who possess land to the extent of 0.99 acres or less generate only 5.5 per cent and agricultural households possessing land between 1 to 2.49 acres generate only 4 per cent of the total saving generated by agricultural households. The bulk of the total savings of agricultural households is observed to be the contribution of middle and rich farming households. The respective shares of agricultural households possessing land 2.50 to 4.99 acres, 5.00 to 9.99 acres and 10.00 acres and above is 17.9 per cent, 40.9 per cent and 31.9 per cent respectively. As regards the disposal of savings also these households belonging to the upper strata of rural hierarchy use at least a part of their savings for capital expenditure (with varying proportion in households coming under different land possessed group), although in their cases also, the major part of their savings are deposited in banks. It is difficult to generalise why even among the richer section of the farming households initiative to plough back savings to agriculture in the form of capital expenditure or capital formation is lacking. Apart from the lure of assured return which has been indicated earlier, there must be some other constraints which stand in the way of their disposing of savings towards the development of their own agriculture.

Table 4.12: Percentage distribution of total amount saved by pattern of deposits, pattern of use and pattern of advance for each type of villages and households for two districts

Types of villages by districts	Types of households	Pattern of deposits			Pattern of use					Pattern of advance	
		Deposited in banks	Deposited in post office	Deposited to other non-banking financial institutions or other financial institutions	Used for purchasing of land	Used for purchasing of building	Used for purchasing of implements and tools	Used for purchasing of materials for household enterprise, profession etc.	Others	Advanced as loan to friends and relatives	Advanced as loan to others
(1)	(2)	(3)	(4)	(5)	(6)	(7)	(8)	(9)	(10)	(11)	(12)
Bardhaman:											
Villages nearer to town	Agricultural households	56.5	–	–	31.2	–	–	0.8	4.4	7.1	–
	All households	62.8	–	0.2	20.8	–	–	1.6	9.8	4.8	–
Villages remote from town	Agricultural households	76.2	1.7	–	–	–	20.9	–	1.2	–	–
	All households	80.0	1.2	–	–	–	15.5	0.5	2.8	–	–
All villages	Agricultural households	66.1	0.8	–	15.9	–	10.2	0.4	2.9	3.7	–
	All households	70.7	0.6	0.1	11.2	–	7.1	1.1	6.6	2.6	–
South 24-Paraganas:											
Villages nearer to town	Agricultural households	94.4	–	–	–	–	–	–	5.6	–	–
	All households	92.9	–	–	–	–	–	–	7.1	–	–
Villages remote from town	Agricultural households	89.4	1.5	–	7.6	–	–	–	1.5	–	–
	All households	92.6	0.8	–	3.6	–	–	0.7	1.9	0.4	–
All villages	Agricultural households	91.8	0.8	–	3.9	–	–	–	3.5	–	–
	All households	92.7	0.4	–	1.9	–	–	0.4	4.4	0.2	–

Table 4.13: Percentage distribution of total household savings by principal occupation of households and the distribution of savings of households in each principal occupation group by types of disposals

Districts: Combined all villages

Principal occupation of households	*Amount saved (Rs.)*	*Percentage of total amount saved*	*Pattern of deposits*			*Pattern of use*					*Pattern of advance*		*Total*
			Deposited in banks	*Deposited in post office*	*Deposited to other non-banking financial institutions or other financial institutions*	*Used for purchasing of land*	*Used for purchasing of building*	*Used for purchasing of implements and tools*	*Used for purchasing of materials for household enterprise, profession etc.*	*Others*	*Advanced as loan to friends and relatives*	*Advanced as loan to others*	
(1)	(2)	(3)	(4)	(5)	(6)	(7)	(8)	(9)	(10)	(11)	(12)	(13)	(14)
1. Agriculture and allied activities	376340	61.2	74.3	0.8	–	11.7	–	6.6	0.3	3.9	2.4	–	100.0
2. Manu. including industrial servicing	52734	8.6	85.0	0.1	0.8	–	–	–	4.3	9.8	–	–	100.0
3. Trading	143150	23.3	94.0	–	0.1	–	–	–	1.0	4,.5	0.4	–	100.0
4. Construction including construction workers	8000	1.3	–	–	–	–	–	–	–	100.0	–	–	100.0
5. Transport operation including small transport operators	10512	1.7	95.2	–	–	–	–	–	–	4.8	–	–	100.0
6. Personal and other services	23600	3.8	100.0	–	–	–	–	–	–	–	–	–	100.0
All	6143336	100.0	80.2	0.5	0.1	7.2	–	4.1	0.8	5.6	1.5	–	100.0

Table 4.14: Percentage distribution of amount saved by the agricultural households by different types of disposal and by household land possessed group

Districts: Combined all villages													
			Pattern of deposits			*Pattern of use*					*Pattern of advance*		
Land possessed group (acres)	*Amount saved (Rs.)*	*Percentage of total amount saved*	*Deposited in banks*	*Deposited in post office*	*Deposited to other non-banking financial institutions or other financial institutions*	*Used for purchasing of land*	*Used for purchasing of building*	*Used for purchasing of implements and tools*	*Used for purchasing of materials for household enterprise, profession etc.*	*Others*	*Advanced as loan to friends and relatives*	*Advanced as loan to others*	*Total*
(1)	(2)	(3)	(4)	(5)	(6)	(7)	(8)	(9)	(10)	(11)	(12)	(13)	(14)
1. 0.01 – 0.49	500	0.1	–	–	–	–	–	–	–	100.0	–	–	100.0
2. 0.50 – 0.99	20000	5.4	–	–	–	45.0	–	–	–	10.0	45.0	–	100.0
3. 1.00 – 2.49	15000	4.0	100.0	–	–	–	–	–	–	–	–	–	100.0
4. 2.50 – 4.99	66790	17.9	84.3	3.0	–	–	–	–	1.5	11.2	–	–	100.0
5. 5.00 – 9.99	151950	40.7	82.5	–	–	3.3	13.2	–	–	1.0	–	–	100.0
6. 10.00 and above	119100	31.9	69.8	0.3	–	25.2	4.2	–	–	–	–	–	100.0
All	373340	100.0	74.9	0.3	–	11.8	6.7	–	0.3	3.1	2.4	–	100.0

Extent of Household Indebtedness and Nature of Credit Market

Needless to say that credit plays an important role in agricultural economy. Attempt has been made in the case study to collect information on the extent of indebtedness of the households surveyed, on the amount of credit transacted during the year ending on the date of survey and the rate of interest charged for the loan advanced. The collected information have been summarised and presented in Tables 4.15, 4.16 and 4.17. The data reveals that in regard to the different characteristics of indebtedness, the position of households in Bardhaman is different from that in South 24-Paraganas. While the proportion of indebted households to the total number of households surveyed in both the districts is observed to be almost of a similar order (36%), all the other characteristics relevant to the operation of credit and the nature of credit market appear to be different in two districts. Whereas in Bardhaman, the dominance of indigenous moneylenders and non-government financial agencies is on the wane, the banks replacing them to take the dominant position (68.5% of household is observed to be indebted to banks), the former continues to have their sway in the credit market in South 24-Paraganas (63.3% of households are reported to be indebted to individual money-lenders of non-government financial agencies). Again whereas the number of small creditors are very large (78% of indebted households reported having taken loan of Rs.5,000 or less) in South 24-Paraganas, the number of small debtors is relatively less in Bardhaman (57.4% of indebted households). It may be seen that households taking loan which lies within the range Rs. 5,001-50,000 and in the next higher range 50,001-1,00,000 are almost of equal size in Bardhaman (20% of indebted households in each case). The situation is understandable as the households covered in the case study in Bardhaman are observed to be in economically higher off position than those of South 24-Paraganas.

Table 4.15: Percentage of indebted households to total households and percentage distribution of indebted households by nature of indebtedness

District	Nature of indebtedness					
	Percentage of indebted households	*Households indebted to bank*	*Households indebted to some non-banking financial institutions*	*Households indebted to some non-banking indigenous agency*	*Households indebted to some relation or friends*	*All*
(1)	(2)	(3)	(4)	(5)	(6)	(7)
South 24-Paraganas	36.7	34.6	3.6	20.0	41.8	100.0
Bardhaman	36.0	68.5	7.4	5.6	18.5	100.0

Table 4.16: Percentage of indebted households by value of indebtedness group

District	Value of debt group (Rs.)							
	Upto 500	*501–1000*	*1001–2000*	*2001–5000*	*5001–10000*	*10000–50000*	*500001 & above*	*All*
(1)	(2)	(3)	(4)	(5)	(6)	(7)	(8)	(9)
South 24-Paraganas	10.9	5.5	21.8	40.0	14.6	3.6	3.6	100.0
Bardhaman	9.2	12.9	14.8	20.4	20.4	20.4	1.9	100.0

Table 4.17: Average rate of interest group (Rs.) paid by individual households

District	Average rate of interest group (Rs.)							
	Upto 10%	*10% > upto 15%*	*15% > upto 20%*	*20% > upto 39%*	*39% & more*	*Mortgage of land etc.*	*Interest free*	*All*
(1)	(2)	(3)	(4)	(5)	(6)	(7)	(8)	(9)
South 24-Paraganas	14.5	30.9	3.6	7.3	16.4	5.5	21.8	100.0
Bardhaman	24.0	59.3	3.7	3.7	–	–	9.3	100.0

Capital Expenditure and Capital Formation

Apparently, it may appear odd to present and discuss at the fag end of this chapter, the data on capital expenditure incurred by households in agricultural and non-agricultural enterprises and the formation of capital assets therein collected in the household survey conducted in the case study villages as ascertaining the nature and characteristics of capital expenditure and capital formation in agricultural economy is the central theme of the present study. But we consider the sequencing of the topics of discussion made in the foregoing on the status, scale and structure of the household enterprises and also on the general economic fabric of the households covered in the survey it is in order that they are expected to provide appropriate background materials for a better appreciation and appraisal of the nature of capital expenditure and capital formation in household enterprises as are revealed from the household survey data. In the following, first the position of stock of household asset-holding including the holding of capital stock expressed in terms of value of asset-holding at current prices followed by an analysis the flow of asset-holding, i.e. expenditure incurred towards purchase or acquiring of such assets expressed in the same manner in terms of value at current prices will be discussed.

Stock of Household Asset

Information on the value at current prices of stock of household assets including capital assets possessed by households as on date of survey have been collected in the survey from each of the household interviewed in the survey. The summarised data are presented in Table 4.18. It may be seen from the table that of total value of household asset-holding, the value of land and residential buildings constitutes, (expressed in terms of percentage proportion) the major bulk of household assets-holding. This generalisation holds good for all households irrespective of nearness or remoteness of the villages from urban centres and also irrespective of the two different districts from where two sets of households (from two sets of villages) have been selected for the survey. The proportion of the value of land and residential building to the total value of household asset-holdings is observed to have varied between 76 to 91 per cent. This wide divergence in proportion is due to the different conditions obtaining in the two different types of villages selected and also due to the varying condition in the two different districts: these are not mere conjectures but comes out clearly from the data shown in Table 4.18. District-wise picture is, however, very clear. Whereas this average value of the stock of land and building in South 24-Paraganas is about 87 per cent of total value of household asset-holding, in Bardhaman, the corresponding proportion is 75 per cent.

In view of the fact that land and residential building, among other household asset-holdings occupy a dominant position in the rural scene in both the districts, logically the share of the stock of other capital assets, namely, buildings for farm or non-farm business, draught animals, implements and tools etc., is bound to be very small in both the districts. Comparing the two sets of figures shown in the table, it may be seen that the situation in Bardhaman is relatively better than that in South 24-Paraganas. Whereas in Bardhaman, the average value of the stock of capital assets, taking all the household sampled in two different types of villages in the district together, is about 16 per cent of the total value of the stock of household asset-holding, in the case of South 24-Paraganas the corresponding proportion is only 7 per cent. If we consider, each of the items of capital stock separately, the niggardly condition in regard to the use of capital assets both in farm and non-farm business becomes more clear, the situation in Bardhaman, though, is better than South 24-Paraganas. Even for draught animal, the situation is hardly believable, as the proportion of value of the stock of draught animal is only about 1 per cent in South 24-Paraganas and about 2.4 per cent is Bardhaman.

However, dismal may be the picture portrayed above, the situation is understandable if we consider the size distribution of total land owned of the surveyed households in either of the two districts. From the data on the size distribution of household ownership holding shown earlier in this chapter, it may be observed that more than 50 per cent of the total number of households covered in the survey in each of the two districts are either marginal or small holders. The owners of medium size-holding, i.e. those owning land holding size between 2.50 acres and 7.49 acres constitute about 22.0 per cent of the total ownership holdings of households covered in the survey in Bardhaman and 31.3 per cent in South 24-Paraganas. The large holders, i.e. those households owning land-holding between 7.50 acres and 19.99 acres constitute 11.7 per cent and 6.7 per cent of the total ownership holding respectively in Bardhaman and South 24-Paraganas. So, even if the money required for the purchase of other than traditional capital assets become affordable to households, they will hesitate to go in for the venture as, given the tiny holding they either own or possess, the application of non-traditional capital assets may turn out to be uneconomical and thus they generally opt first to acquire more land instead of other capital equipments including draught animals. They also perhaps always think of utilising more of their idle household manpower than to substitute them by improved tools or implements. About non-farm business also, considering the scale of non-farm business the households run indicated by their value of annual turn over, it becomes evident that barring a few, most of the non-farm enterprises are too small to afford maintaining large stock of capital assets other than land for non-farm use (for a large number of enterprises perhaps apart of the residential purposes, houses are used for household enterprise) and only less costly tools, implements and fixtures for the non-farm business. In value terms, therefore, they generally constitute only a negligible or small proportion of the total value of the stock of asset-holding.

Flow of Household Capital Expenditure

Data on the value of all capital expenditure at current prices incurred by the households during the period of 365 days ending on the date of survey, i.e. the money value of the purchase made outright or expenditure incurred for construction, major repair, improvements or additions of different capital items, such as land, buildings, implements or tools, machineries, orchard, livestock and poultry birds, water bodies etc., during the period of reference have been collected in the household survey. Also collected in the survey are the information on the expenditure incurred by the household on normal repair and maintenance of any or all capital items listed above for maintaining them intact for their productive use in household agriculture or non-agricultural enterprises. It was seen earlier, while defining capital expenditure and capital formation, that expenditure incurred or purchase of land and old building and on normal repair and maintenance of capital items are treated as capital expenditure. They cannot strictly be called expenditure for capital formation. But expenditure on all other items listed above are to be included under capital expenditure as well as expenditure for capital formation.

In Table 4.19, the summarised data on capital expenditure flow, during the one year period preceding the date of survey, collected in the household survey are presented. The data are presented for two districts separately by combining all households selected from two different types of villages in each district. This has been done as otherwise the number of total sample households would have been too small to distribute between 14 or 15 capital items. It may be seen that data are also presented separately for two sets of households—one having agriculture as their principal household occupation and the other with non-agricultural activity as their principal household occupation. Excepting the capital items land and buildings and normal repair and maintenance, all other items are shown separately under two categories—(i) used for farm business and (ii) used for non-farm business.

Since, the data on the flow of capital expenditure obtained from the household survey relate only to a period of one year and comparable results for at least another two or three preceding or succeeding years are not available, it will be difficult to generalise, on the basis of these data, about the trend for the contemporary period, of the relative proportion of allocation of total capital expenditure incurred by households on different capital items purchased, constructed, improved through major repair etc., for household productive enterprises. But nevertheless from the two sets of data presented here—one on the value of capital stock and the other on the value of capital flow, one can perhaps have a very general perception as regards the relative importance attached to different items of capital expenditure by households strictly under the given condition obtaining in the survey villages in the two districts. We want to only emphasise that before interpreting the data one should be aware of their limitation.

The data shown in Table 4.19 are quite revealing and hardly there is any scope for discussion for further elucidation of the position regarding the flow of capital assets during the period of reference in the households brought under the survey coverage. Only a few important feature of capital expenditure incurred by households are highlighted below.

It may be observed that both for households with agriculture as principal occupation and also for households with non-agricultural activities as principal occupation in Bardhaman as well as South 24-Paraganas, the major share of the total value of capital expenditure during the reference year are incurred on account of normal repair and maintenance of capital assets in possession of households. The respective percentage proportions of total capital expenditure in agricultural and non-agricultural households spent on normal repair and maintenance in Bardhaman and South 24-Paraganas are 58.98, 45.24, 40.93 and 46.26. The next important item for which households in both the districts spend a substantial amount is major repair, improvements and alterations of residential plots, buildings, houses, etc., and the amount is proportionately higher in non-agricultural households than in agricultural households. The overriding importance attached by households for acquiring and for improvement and extension of land and buildings becomes

Table 4.18: Percentage of the value of different types of asset holding to total value of asset holding at current prices

District	Type of village	Asset-holding category													
		Land for house site and land used for cultivation, other agri. act. or other non-agri. act. and other land	*Residential building*	*Building used for farm business*	*Building used for non-farm business*	*Machinery, tools and implements*	*Furniture and fixture for farm and non-farm business*	*Transport equipments*	*Household equipment (excluding furniture and fixtures)*	*Furniture and fixture for household use*	*Household utensils and wares*	*Ornaments and jewellery*	*Financial asset*	*Domestic animal and draught animal*	*All*
(1)	(2)	(3)	(4)	(5)	(6)	(7)	(8)	(9)	(10)	(11)	(12)	(13)	(14)	(15)	(16)
South 24-Paraganas	Nearer to town	75.10	16.22	0.72	2.17	1.42	0.15	0.43	0.50	0.61	0.23	0.70	1.15	0.60	100.00
	Remote from town	63.61	21.01	2.25	2.62	1.07	0.18	0.75	0.53	1.00	0.30	2.21	3.19	1.28	100.00
	All	69.33	18.62	1.49	2.40	1.25	0.17	0.59	0.51	0.31	0.26	1.45	2.18	0.94	100.00
Bardhaman	Nearer to town	44.39	26.70	5.59	2.67	4.62	0.36	2.60	1.46	1.55	0.75	3.85	3.02	2.44	100.00
	Remote from town	55.56	22.38	1.81	2.33	5.53	0.15	1.37	0.83	1.00	0.37	3.52	2.83	2.32	100.00
	All	50.84	24.20	3.41	2.47	5.15	0.24	1.89	1.10	1.23	0.53	3.66	2.91	2.37	100.00
All	Nearer to town	61.45	20.88	2.89	2.39	2.34	0.24	1.39	0.93	1.03	0.46	2.10	1.98	1.42	100.00
	Remote from town	59.42	21.72	2.02	2.47	3.39	0.16	1.08	0.69	1.00	0.33	2.89	3.01	1.82	100.00
	All	60.36	21.33	2.42	2.43	3.14	0.20	1.22	0.80	1.01	0.39	2.53	2.53	1.64	100.00

Table 4.19: Percentage of capital expenditure by items of total capital expenditure incurred by households for Bardhaman and South 24-Paraganas

Items of capital expenditure	*Bardhaman*		*South 24-Paraganas*	
	All households with principal occupation agriculture	*All households with principal occupation non-agril.*	*All households with principal occupation agriculture*	*All households with principal occupation non-agril.*
(1)	(2)	(3)	(4)	(5)
1. Additional improvements, major repair or alteration of residential plots, houses and buildings	12.27	38.52	23.97	27.28
For farm–business				
2. Reclamation of land	0.62	1.59	1.12	2.34
3. New plantation, orchard and annual planting	–	–	0.05	–
4. Construction, addition, major repair & alteration of farm houses, barns, animal sheds etc.	5.07	0.23	2.41	1.34
5. New construction, additions to wells, tubewells etc. and major repairs	1.88	–	0.49	–
6. New pumpset, major repairs and addition of pumpsets	8.45	0.17	5.06	–
7. New agricultural implements, machinery and major repair thereof	6.99	0.11	17.08	0.32
8. Livestock and poultry	4.09	2.45	7.07	5.05
9. New water areas, ponds and extension of old water areas, fishing nets, tools and major repairs thereof	0.29	–	0.91	–

(*Contd.*)

Table 4.19: (*Contd.*)

(1)	(2)	(3)	(4)	(5)
10. Implement and tools, major repair and maintenance and allied activities including sericulture	-	-	0.02	-
For non-farm business				
11. Improvement of land, major repair and maintenance of building used for manufacturing	-	3.57	0.44	0.57
12. New implements, tools, other accessories, furnitures, fittings and major repair and maintenance thereof	0.98	4.80	0.65	13.76
13. Transport equipments—new items, major additions, improvement and production at household	0.08	2.83	-	3.08
14. Normal repair and maintenance for all items included above	58.98	45.24	40.73	46.26
15. Land and building for farm business	0.30	0.49	-	-
All	100.00	100.00	100.00	100.00

apparent from data on stock of household assets and also flow of capital asset shown in Tables 4.18 and 4.19.

The data reveal that apart from the large portion of the total amount of capital expenditure that is incurred by households on major repair, improvements and extension of residential plots, houses and buildings which undoubtedly is the expenditure for formation of capital assets, another 20-25 per cent of total capital expenditure is incurred by agricultural household for the purchase of capital assets, namely, irrigation equipments like pumpsets, agricultural machineries etc., which are used as direct aid for the development of agriculture and thus help formation of tangible capital asset for household agricultural enterprise. The variation in percentage noted is, obviously, due to varying situation obtaining in the two districts. But in the case of non-agricultural households, the proportion of total capital expenditure spent for the purchase of capital assets, such as, implements, tools etc., for non-agricultural enterprises, transport equipment etc., thereby forming tangible capital asset for the household non-agricultural enterprises is comparatively very small. It is only about 8 per cent in Bardhaman and about 16 per cent in South 24-Paraganas.

Although it is difficult to derive any firm conclusion regarding the nature of capital expenditure and capital formation in both agricultural and non-agricultural households in the surveyed households in the two districts on the basis of the results of one snap-shot enquiry, it can nevertheless be surmised, having considered the overall condition of the economic environment in which the household enterprises, both agricultural and non-agricultural, operate, that the households try to spend as little as absolutely essential to only keep the enterprise running. At least for the non-agricultural enterprises this observation can be made with more confidence. In fine, it may be concluded that the idea of development and entrepreneurial initiative to engineer that seems to be lacking everywhere. It is quite possible that the compelling limiting factors which have been mentioned earlier have set the observed behaviour pattern of average households with regard to development and whatever development initiatives are taken remain limited to richer households having bigger size of land-holding—either owned or possessed.

Note

1. NSS 43rd Round (July, 1987 - June, 1988)—the 4th quinquennial survey on consumer expenditure.

5

Deposit and Credit Flow from Banks in Rural Areas of Bardhaman and South 24-Paraganas

An Examination into Lead Bank's Ledger and Official Records

In the preceding chapter, we have briefly discussed the pattern of household disbursements, savings and indebtedness based on the data collected from the rural households covered in the survey conducted in a number of selected villages in Bardhaman and South 24-Paraganas.

A summary of the discussion is given as follows:

(i) About a half of the agricultural households (53 per cent in Bardhaman and 43 per cent in South 24-Paraganas) reported to have made saving during the reference years.

(ii) Among the total number of selected households having agriculture and allied activities as principal occupation in all the selected villages in two districts Bardhaman and 24-Paraganas, taken together, only the households possessing middle (5 acres to 9.99 acres) and large (10 acres and above) land-holding size make some savings. Of the small and marginal holders, the former saves only a small amount, the latter makes negligible savings.

(iii) Of the total amount of money saved 70 per cent and 49 per cent come from agricultural households respectively in Bardhaman and South 24-Paraganas.

(iv) Of the total amount saved by agriculturist 66 per cent

and 92 per cent is deposited by the households respectively in Bardhaman and South 24-Paraganas.

(v) Both in Bardhaman and South 24-Paraganas villages, the proportion of indebted households is little over one-third of the total number of households surveyed, one-third and two-third of them in South 24-Paraganas and Bardhaman villages respectively are observed to be indebted to banks.

(vi) While in South 24-Paraganas, a large proportion of households (more than 75 per cent) reported to have taken loan of small amount (less than Rs. 5000), in Bardhaman the proportion of small (less than Rs. 5000) and large (Rs. 5000 and above) amount of loan getters are almost equally distributed.

Apprehending that the above information which has been obtained from a small number of households from only a few selected villages of the two districts may not reflect a realistic pattern of deposit and credit flow in the area, an effort has been made to probe into the official records of at least a few branches of the lead banks operating in the respective areas of the two districts (where the household survey has been conducted) so that, data forthcoming from the probe may supply further supplementary information regarding the pattern of deposit and credit flow in the area to and from banks to the rural households in the area.

With a view to promoting comprehensive agricultural and other rural development programme, the role of commercial and other development banks, in providing the required credit support to the rural population is well-known. Since 1980 with the inception of 'service area approach' of new credit policy initiated by the Reserve Bank of India which encouraged the shift from 'Class' approach to 'Mass' approach in regard to the rural credit, a new orientation was given to the formulation of Annual Credit Plans of different banks and each bank is trying to conform to this objective laid out by the Reserve Bank of India.

As a part of this study, the probes into the official records of the two lead banks, the UBI and UCO operating respectively in the districts of South 24-Paraganas and Bardhaman was undertaken by our trained investigator for about 3 months, of which one month was spent for contacting appropriate officials, both at district headquarters and also at the offices of a few branches of the lead banks operating in the different police station areas where the main household survey was conducted.

Two types of data have been collected through this probing enquiry, they are:

(a) The data on the aggregated amount of credit as well as deposit for the entire district have been compiled from the record official document for each district maintained at the district headquarter of the concerned lead bank. It contains the accounts of all the banks both commercial and other operating in the districts. The data refer to 1987, 1988, 1989, and 1990.

(b) In addition to the above data, the data on deposit flow from individual rural households have been collected from the bank's ledger or account opening forms maintained in each of the branches of the lead banks selected and for obtaining such data special permission has been obtained from the office of the district headquarter of the lead bank. For collecting data on deposit flow either from the bank's ledger or the account opening forms, only 5 per cent of the total number of depositors have been covered and the entries recorded for four or five calendar years have been copied. Since the banks are not permitted, by law, to divulge the information regarding names, address and amount deposited to anybody, only the occupation of the depositor have been collected. From these information, therefore, only the trend of the growth of deposit by occupation of the depositor could be ascertained.

Trend of Deposit Flow to Bank by Occupation of Depositor

In Table 5.1, the summarised version of the compiled data

obtained from bank's ledger is given. Only the data for two calendar years 1986 and 1990 have been presented in the Table. In regard to the pattern of deposit flow to bank from the rural households, two important features clearly emerge out from the data presented. They are:

(a) For both the districts, among all the depositors, Businessmen and Cultivators are found to be the two major depositors. This has been observed in all the branches of the banks from where the data have been compiled.

(b) Having compared the figures of two calendar years shown in the Table, it is observed that excepting in a few branches in South 24-Paraganas, in all other branches of banks, both in South 24-Paraganas and Bardhaman, the relative position of cultivators as depositors has been observed to be rising and that of traders and businessmen declining. Based on these data one need not however, make any generalisation for the state as a whole as the data relates only to a small area of the state and only for a few years, but the feature that increasing number of cultivators are coming to the banks to deposit a part of the total amount of their savings may, particularly, be noted as this may be considered a signal of change of the saving investment behaviour of at least the upper strata of the cultivating community who, as the household survey data reveals, seem to be the emerging entrepreneurial class in the rural agricultural economy in the sense that this section of cultivators, particularly this section of cultivators have been observed to be taking concrete and positive steps to change the capital structure of their household farm business.

Sector-wise Credit Flow Performance by Commercial and Other Banks

Having probed into the official records on the performance

of different banks in advancing credit for rural development works in a district in agriculture, small scale industries and other services for different calendar years maintained by the concerned lead bank of the district, a summary compilation has been made. The summarised data are presented in Table 5.2. In this table, for a particular year, the targeted amount of credit to be advanced for the different sectors of development activity, the amount of credit actually advanced and the percentage rate of performance are shown for a number of years separately for the lead bank, other commercial banks and other banks operating in the two districts are shown. By 'Other Banks' meant the Gramin Bank, The Co-operative Credit Bank etc.

The overall impression that one can draw from the data presented in the Table are as follows:

(a) Taking the total amount of credit together purported to be advanced by different banks in different years, the flow of credit, both in Bardhaman and South 24-Paraganas, do not show a upward rise. Whereas over the specified years a steady decline of amount is clearly visible in the case of South 24-Paraganas, the amount of credit goes up and again comes down in the case of Bardhaman.

(b) Both for Bardhaman and South 24-Paraganas, the amount of credit allocation for agriculture is observed to be generally higher compared to that allocated respectively for small scale industries and services.

(c) Whereas for Bardhaman, the amount of targeted allocation of credit for agriculture is found to be high and rising over few years prior to 1990-91, for South 24-Paraganas it is less than one-third of that allocated for Bardhaman for every year and also found to be declining steadily with a sudden fall in 1989.

(d) In regard to the achievement in agricultural sector measured in terms of performance rate (amount achieved ÷ amount targeted × 100), the rate differs from bank to bank, though the 'Other Banks' clearly exhibit

> their better performance compared to the performance of either 'Lead Bank' or 'Other Commercial Bank'. It is interesting to note that in so far as the disbursement of rural credit is concerned, the lead bank does not really lead. Their position, in most of the years, in both the districts is third, the second position having been occupied by 'Other Commercial Banks' and the first position, as has been stated above is occupied by the 'Other Banks'.

Assuming that a prior knowledge about the limits and constraints standing in the way of smooth implementation of annual credit plan in the rural areas were available to the banks and particularly the lead bank before they fix and finalise the targeted amount of credit to be disbursed in a year, the reasons for the gap between the allocated target amount of credit and the actual amount of credit disbursed, which perpetuates over the years and also widens in some years are difficult to explain as we are not possessed with the other relevant information. Most probably, the anticipated growth of infrastructure, such as, opening up of new branches of banks, the augmentation of manpower etc., required for the implementation of the credit plan did not, meanwhile, materialise. One reason, among other important reasons, might be the disquieting feature of the rural credit market reflected in the very low credit repayment rate and any sign for their upward movement was not discernible.

But as opposed to a rather conservative and cautious attitude towards disbursement of credit in rural areas adopted by 'Lead Banks' and 'Other Commercial Banks', 'Other Banks' seem to have taken a relatively liberal view which gets reflected in their performance rate in all the years for which the data are presented. It is likely that those 'Other Banks' are constrained to take such a different view in the matter of disbursement of credit as they have often to satisfy the wishes of different powerful pressure groups operating in rural areas.

Table 5.1: Percentage of number of accounts by occupations of depositors

Local bank	P.S.	Local bank branches selected	Year	Occupation of depositors													
				Businessman	Cultivator	Teacher	Service	Doctor	Advocate	Labourer	Housewife	Student	Retired persons	Unemployed	Others	Not available	Total
(1)	(2)	(3)	(4)	(5)	(6)	(7)	(8)	(9)	(10)	(11)	(12)	(13)	(14)	(15)	(16)	(17)	(18)
				District : South 24-Paraganas													
UBI	Jainagar	Bahara	1986	44.0	16.0	–	8.0	–	–	–	28.0	4.0	–	–	–	–	100.0
			1990	35.6	8.1	3.7	15.6	–	–	–	22.2	11.1	2.2	–	–	1.5	100.0
		Dosha	1986	–	42.9	–	–	–	–	–	57.1	–	–	–	–	–	100.0
			1990	10.3	56.4	5.1	5.1	–	–	–	18.0	3.8	–	–	–	1.3	100.0
		Raidighi	1986	42.9	23.8	9.5	4.8	–	–	9.5	9.5	–	–	–	–	–	100.0
			1990	24.7	38.3	8.5	5.9	–	–	2.6	12.3	4.5	–	–	–	3.2	100.0
	Mograhat	Sirakola	1986	30.2	18.6	4.7	14.0	–	–	–	11.6	7.0	–	2.3	–	11.6	100.0
			1990	24.6	22.3	3.3	17.5	–	0.5	4.3	14.7	5.7	0.9	0.5	–	5.7	100.0
		Shri Chandrahat	1989	30.0	20.0	10.0	10.0	–	–	–	–	30.0	–	–	–	–	100.0
			1990	21.3	13.3	17.4	22.7	1.3	1.3	–	10.7	8.0	–	–	–	4.0	100.0
		Mograhat	1986	13.8	27.6	13.8	6.9	–	–	3.4	17.3	3.4	–	3.4	–	13.4	100.0
			1990	19.6	21.2	16.8	11.4	–	–	4.3	17.9	2.2	0.6	0.6	–	0.4	100.0
		Kalash	1990	36.8	12.3	8.8	8.8	–	–	1.8	17.5	10.5	–	–	–	3.5	100.0
		Banipur	1990	30.2	28.3	–	9.4	1.9	1.9	–	13.2	13.2	–	–	–	1.9	100.0

(Contd.)

Table 5.1: (*Contd.*)

(1)	(2)	(3)	(4)	(5)	(6)	(7)	(8)	(9)	(10)	(11)	(12)	(13)	(14)	(15)	(16)	(17)	(18)
		Mondi	1988	16.2	14.7	5.9	14.7	–	–	–	25.0	7.4	–	–	–	16.1	100.0
			1990-91	16.1	17.3	4.2	19.6	–	0.6	0.6	25.6	7.1	–	–	–	8.9	100.0
	Bishnupur	Pailan	1986	21.6	27.0	2.7	21.6	–	–	–	16.3	2.7	2.7	–	–	5.4	100.0
			1990-91	16.2	16.2	2.6	31.8	–	–	0.7	19.5	5.8	2.6	0.7	–	3.9	100.0
		Amtala	1987	24.4	20.0	–	15.6	–	–	6.7	11.1	11.1	–	2.2	–	8.9	100.0
			1990	27.9	9.4	3.8	22.3	–	–	3.0	14.7	7.2	4.5	0.8	0.4	6.0	100.0
		Mamudpur	1989	35.7	7.2	4.8	11.9	–	–	–	21.4	16.7	–	–	–	2.3	100.0
			1990-91	34.0	5.2	10.3	15.5	1.0	–	1.0	18.6	11.4	1.0	1.0	–	1.0	100.0
District : Bardhaman																	
	Galsi	Budbud	1986-87	21.7	4.4	4.4	30.4	–	–	4.3	34.8	–	–	–	–	–	100.0
			1990	12.4	26.8	1.0	20.6	–	–	0.5	36.1	2.1	–	–	–	0.5	100.0
UCO	Bhatar	Bhatar	1988	21.4	21.4	14.3	28.6	–	–	–	7.2	–	7.1	–	–	–	100.0
			1990-91	23.0	28.7	3.5	24.1	–	–	–	10.4	4.6	4.6	–	–	1.1	100.0
		Mahachanda	1986	9.1	40.9	–	27.3	–	–	4.5	9.1	4.6	–	–	4.5	–	100.0
			1990	9.3	43.0	–	26.7	1.2	–	3.4	10.5	4.7	–	–	1.2	–	100.0
	Bardhaman	Baje	1986-87	24.0	8.0	8.0	36.0	–	–	4.0	12.0	8.0	–	–	–	–	100.0
		Pratapur	1990-91	19.6	10.1	2.6	31.2	–	–	4.2	21.7	5.8	3.7	–	–	1.1	100.0
		Alamganj	1986-87	–	–	–	5.0	–	–	65.0	20.0	–	–	–	–	10.0	100.0
			1989-91	19.3	–	2.4	22.9	–	–	25.3	19.3	4.8	–	–	–	6.0	100.0
	Katwa	Kalna	1989-90	33.3	–	–	12.5	–	–	–	20.8	–	4.2	–	–	29.2	100.0
			1990-91	23.1	5.1	5.1	15.4	–	–	–	15.4	2.6	2.6	–	–	30.7	100.0

Source: (1) Annual Credit Plan, 1990-91, United Bank of India, 24-Paraganas (South), Regional Office, South 24-Paraganas District.

(2) Annual Credit Plan, 1990-91, UCO Bank, Fancy Market, Bardhaman, Bardhaman District.

Table 5.2: Bank-wise/Sector-wise review of AAP-1987, 1988, 1989, 1990 (*in Rs. Lakhs*)

Year	Name of banks	Agriculture			Industry			Service			Total		
		Target	Achieved	%	Target	Achieved	%	Target	Achieved	%	Target	Achieved	%
(1)	(2)	(3)	(4)	(5)	(6)	(7)	(8)	(9)	(10)	(11)	(12)	(13)	(14)
	District : South 24-Parganas												
1987	UBI	603.70	344.50	57.06	259.80	230.95	88.55	318.70	267.60	83.97	1182.20	842.15	71.24
	Other Comm. Banks	739.30	566.90	76.68	614.30	462.25	75.35	889.10	635.79	71.51	2242.70	1665.54	74.24
	Other Banks	225.00	217.12	96.50	210.00	310.65	147.93	5.00	2.00	40.00	440.00	529.77	120.40
	Total	1568.00	1128.52	71.97	1084.10	1003.55	92.57	1212.80	905.39	74.65	3864.90	3037.46	78.96
1988	UBI	578.60	281.68	48.68	253.85	168.68	66.45	308.55	217.11	70.36	1141.00	667.47	58.50
	Other Comm. Banks	778.05	532.01	68.38	627.30	560.76	89.39	885.85	620.92	70.09	2291.20	1713.69	74.83
	Other Banks	51.20	44.00	85.94	206.00	317.69	154.22	–	–	–	257.20	361.69	140.63
	Total	1407.85	857.69	60.92	1087.15	1047.13	96.32	1194.40	838.03	70.16	3689.40	2742.85	74.34
1989	UBI	144.65	68.73	47.51	63.46	55.58	87.58	77.14	41.13	53.31	285.25	165.44	58.00
	Other Comm. Banks	190.43	165.96	87.15	160.41	149.31	93.08	226.45	227.75	100.57	577.29	543.02	94.06
	Other Banks	12.80	32.00	250.00	51.50	71.26	138.37	–	–	–	64.30	103.26	160.59
	Total	347.88	266.69	76.66	275.37	276.15	100.28	303.59	268.88	88.57	926.84	811.72	87.58
1990	UBI	394.04	360.28	91.43	279.20	241.25	86.40	273.00	250.49	91.75	946.24	852.02	90.03
	Other Comm. Banks	947.75	505.78	53.37	496.30	495.34	92.55	621.80	644.74	103.69	2065.85	1609.86	77.93
	Other Banks	76.10	36.85	48.42	451.75	307.08	67.98	3.60	0.57	15.83	531.45	344.50	64.82
	Total	1417.89	902.91	63.68	1227.25	1007.67	82.11	898.40	895.80	99.71	3543.54	2806.38	79.20

(*Contd.*)

Table 5.2: (*Contd.*)

(1)	(2)	(3)	(4)	(5)	(6)	(7)	(8)	(9)	(10)	(11)	(12)	(13)	(14)
						District : Bardhaman							
1987	UCO	600.90	130.90	21.78	217.10	30.10	13.86	185.80	99.79	53.71	1003.80	260.79	26.00
	Other Comm. Banks	3030.30	1406.46	46.41	2579.15	1059.35	41.07	2190.35	1110.48	50.70	7799.80	3576.29	45.85
	Other Banks	1404.50	1313.19	93.50	261.70	434.70	162.29	319.50	151.60	47.45	1985.70	1889.49	95.15
	Total	5035.70	2850.55	56.61	3057.95	1514.15	49.52	2695.65	1361.87	50.52	10789.30	5726.57	53.08
1988	UCO	618.50	183.08	29.60	270.00	98.10	36.33	260.00	116.83	44.93	1148.50	398.01	34.65
	Other Comm. Banks	3014.50	1586.37	52.62	2780.00	1363.77	49.06	2542.00	1937.54	76.22	8336.50	4887.68	58.63
	Other Banks	1585.00	1446.00	91.23	450.00	514.88	114.42	480.00	442.52	92.19	2515.00	2403.40	95.56
	Total	5218.00	3215.45	61.62	3500.00	1976.75	56.48	3282.00	2496.89	76.08	12000.00	7689.09	64.08
1989	UCO	291.30	186.80	64.13	90.06	34.36	38.15	221.38	127.33	57.52	602.74	348.49	57.82
	Other Comm. Banks	3042.83	2044.46	67.19	1190.77	725.88	1728.10	1728.10	1278.55	73.99	5961.70	4048.89	67.92
	Other Banks	2759.18	2027.03	73.46	983.00	999.58	317.00	317.00	322.24	101.65	4059.18	3348.85	82.50
	Total	6093.31	4258.29	69.88	2263.83	1759.82	77.74	2266.48	1728.12	76.25	10623.62	7746.23	72.92

Source: (1) Annual Credit Plan, 1990-91, United Bank of India, 24-Paraganas (South), Regional Office, South 24-Paraganas District.
(2) Annual Credit Plan, 1990-91, UCO Bank, Fancy Market, Bardhaman, Bardhaman District.

Credit-Deposit Ratio

Data on the amount of annual deposit accumulation and credit advanced to and from banks in rural areas and also the respective credit-deposit ratios in different groups of banks for a few years upto 1990 shown in Table 5.3 provide further evidence of the adoption of a rather conservative credit policy, particularly by the commercial banks in transacting rural credit. The low achievement rate in attaining the targeted amount of advance fixed in the Annual Action Plan of banks to offer credit support to different rural development programmes and the low credit deposit ratios of different groups of banks are really the two faces of the same malady of the rural credit market which indirectly puts limit to rural development in general and the development of agriculture in rural areas in particular.

The information on deposits, credits and the credit-deposit ratios presented in Table 5.3 show that in the case of South 24-Paraganas the total amount of deposit has slided down in 1990 compared to that in 1988, but the amount of credit advanced has gone up during the same period and the credit-deposit ratio has also gone up from 28 to near about 38 per cent. In the case of Bardhaman on the other hand all the three, the amount of deposit, the amount of credit advanced and the credit-deposit ratio have been found to have gone up steadily between 1987 and 1989-90.

For South 24-Paraganas we do not have corresponding information regarding 'Other Banks', which, as the data show, clearly contributed in boosting up the credit-deposit ratio from 29 to 32 per cent for the district as a whole as during the same period the credit-deposit ratio of Commercial Banks has shown only an increase of a little more than 2 per cent.

From the two sets of data for the two districts shown above and specially the data relating to other banks available for Bardhaman only, one gets inclined to conclude that the total amount deposited in a year in banks is not the sole determinant of the credit-deposit ratio. It is some other factor or factors which play crucial role in fixing up the said ratios. It may be quite possible that specific condition obtaining in districts, both

Table 5.3: Bank-wise credit and deposit flow and credit-deposit ratios by year

(Amount in crores)

Year	*Name of bank*	*Deposit*	*Credit*	*C/D ratio (%)*
(1)	*(2)*	*(3)*	*(4)*	*(5)*
	District: South 24-Paraganas			
1988	UBI	12608.14	3151.95	24.99
	All commercial banks (14)	35819.71	10167.82	28.38
1989	UBI	12704.88	3348.63	26.35
	All commercial banks (13)	29525.20	9106.83	30.34
1990	UBI	15234.00	4730.00	31.20
	All commercial banks (15)	41340.00	13483.00	32.61
	District: Bardhaman			
1987	1. Commercial banks	769.53	203.36	26.42
	2. B.G.B.	11.86	8.84	74.60
	3. B.C.C.B.	51.85	32.68	63.02
	4. Total	833.24	244.88	29.39
1988	1. Commercial banks	921.18	236.27	25.65
	2. B.G.B.	17.32	11.37	65.65
	3. B.C.C.B.	52.15	33.96	65.12
	4. Total	990.65	281.60	28.43
1989-90	1. Commercial banks	990.08	284.63	28.75
	2. B.G.B.	32.42	14.59	62.30
	3. B.C.C.B.	55.49	47.74	86.03
	4. Total	1068.99	346.96	32.46

in regard to the infrastructure of the banks as well as the credit worthiness of the loan receivers, which ultimately prevails in deciding the credit-deposit ratio of banks in a particular district. But then, why is it becoming possible for other banks operating in the same district to venture adopting a more liberal view in advancing credit compared to that adopted by the lead bank or the other commercial banks? It is because of the fact that on the one hand the commercial banks as a responsible custodian of depositors money cannot afford to involve themselves too much in creating bad debt of an undesirably large amount and on the other the co-operative banks and other rural banks do not hesitate to adopt a more liberal (albeit reckless) policy as besides being pressurised by members of co-operatives who themselves are loan receivers, they are sure that like the case of prodigal sons, the state government and Reserve Bank will always come to their rescue if most of the credit transactions made are for supporting a reasonable and genuine economic pursuit. However, this is an open question which remains unanswered as it is difficult to have data to discuss on other related issues with a view to answering this question squarely.

6

Conclusions and Recommendations

From the data based analysis, made in the foregoing chapters, of the trend of capital expenditure and capital formation in Indian agriculture and its changing pattern certain obvious findings emerge out on some of which we have already made certain observation.

In this chapter, our concluding observation based on those findings are listed first and then our recommendations follow:

Conclusions

1. Till 1950-51, Indian agriculture was predominantly a simple land-labour activity supported by capital investment on bullock and only marginal use of irrigation potential already created in certain areas of the country through government efforts. Percentage of the combined value of investment on land, bullock and irrigation equipment was estimated to be 92.6 per cent of the total value of capital investment of which the share of bullock only was as large as 78.7 per cent.
2. The massive central intervention in the form of injection of huge fund as planned investment in agriculture brought about a series of favourable changes, the combined effect of which was reflected in gradual alteration of the investment climate of agriculture all over the country. The plan investment in agriculture was 31 per cent of the value of total plan outlay in the first plan and the proportion varied from 20-25 per cent in subsequent plans upto the Seventh Plan.
3. The immediate impact of the huge investment made

through several five-year plans and annual plans was a manifold increase of agricultural production and more importantly on the food production. But the fullest benefit of such plan investments could not be accrued in a uniform manner throughout the country. Spectacular results were achieved in some states while in others the achievements were not that impressive. Signs of change, however, could be visible in almost all the major states of the country. The impact was generally of two types:

(a) A general awareness regarding the possibility of break through from the traditional and stagnant agriculture was visible everywhere, i.e., a congenial climate was created. Where the institutional and infrastructural factors, such as, size of landholding, condition of land, marketing and credit facilities etc., were not favourable for a drastic change over, a slow but gradual change of the pattern and structure of capital expenditure and capital formation in farm business could be noticed.

(b) Where the required institutional and infrastructural facilities were already in existence or could be created by taking advantage of the central assistance, the cultivator households went whole hog in making rapid progress towards changing the capital structure and technique of production and in due course change akin to revolution in agriculture was ushered-in.

4. Although both the impacts indicated above, left their imprints in all the major states of the country in varying degrees, the latter variety was found to be more pronounced in some of the northern and western states, categorised by us as Group I states. The former variety of the impacts noted above, however, was observed to be more widespread; in some of eastern and central states its predominance was very clear. We categorised these states as Group II states. Since Group II states

covered a large area and also larger number of cultivator households in the country, the resulting effect of the first impact could easily be imagined.

5. Size of farm-holding, among other important factors, determining the pattern of capital expenditure and capital formation, is the most important and perhaps the key factor. The average size of operational holding in the Group II states, which exhibit only a limping progress in attempting the break through from the traditional pattern of capital investment in agriculture, reported to have varied from 0.4 hectares to only 1.6 hectares in 1980-81. Whereas, the average size of operational holding in the Group I states, where the so-called new agricultural revolution has taken a firm root, is reported to have varied between 1.9 hectares to 4.4 hectares in 1980-81.
6. The quality and the pattern of capital expenditure and capital formation in farm business vary according to the level of economic condition of cultivator households. Assuming the value of household asset-holding as a suitable proxy of household income, households grouped under the asset-holding value below Rs. 5,000 have been categorised by us as low-income households, those coming under the value group Rs. 5,000 to Rs. 15,000 as moderate income household, those coming under Rs. 15,000 to Rs. 30,000 as middle income households and all households coming under the value group Rs. 30,000 and above as high-income households. The analysis shows that:

   (a) capital investment of the low-income households is predominantly of traditional nature, the major portion of investment being made in acquiring more land and on improvement on land.
   (b) the moderate income households lay more emphasis on purchase of irrigation equipments and agricultural implements of traditional nature.
   (c) the middle-income households allocate major

portion of their capital investment only on two capital items—irrigation equipments and agricultural machineries and implements of both traditional and modern types though share of traditional types is of higher value than the modern types.

(d) for the high-income households, more than 70 per cent of their capital items goes for acquiring their own irrigation resources and implements and also for purchasing agricultural machinery of which the share of modern machineries is higher in value than that of the traditional type.

7. It is interesting to note that whether we go by the criterion of the size of household farm-holding or by the value of household asset-holding, the proportion of households, coming under two lower brackets of each one of the two criteria used for classification of cultivator households termed 'marginal and small land holders' in the case of former and 'low and moderate asset-holders' for the latter, is the largest among the cultivator households in rural areas. It is more than 73 per cent, if, the former criterion is used and 88 per cent, if, the latter is used. And, as we find from our analysis, by and large, they constitute the largest bulk of cultivator households which remains tied up with the traditional mode of cultivation and their share in capital expenditure is the lowest.

8. Despite introduction of new rural credit policy and expansion of rural credit facilities by government since sixties, the only distinguishable feature to be noticed is the weakening of the grip of private non-institutional credit agencies on the cultivator community. But in so far as the availability of credit from institutional agencies, only a small segment of the cultivators are benefited. Because of their having lower size of farm-holding and lower size of household asset-holding, a large section of marginal and small cultivators are not considered credit worthy and thus they cannot reap

the advantage of the institutional credit. As a result, some of them have to still depend on private non-institutional credit agencies and suffer and others go for other means to meet their credit requirements. Thus, the utilisation of credit money for development of agriculture, for changing the capital structure of their farm business becomes relevant only for the more well-to-do section of cultivators coming within the middle and big farm-holding or the middle and high household asset-holding bracket. Only a very small proportion of marginal and small cultivators get benefited from institutional credit. But where the credit co-operatives have flourished or where the co-operative banks adopt a more liberal credit policy, the benefit of credit reaches them also. Another feature of rural credit which gets revealed from our analysis is that while the richer section of the cultivators utilise more than half of the credit they secure for improving the capital structure of their farm business, the poorer section utilise more than half of the credit they obtain to meet the consumption need of their households.

9. Having examined the phenomenon of capital expenditure and capital formation in farm business in rural India, its characteristics in different states and also its features revealed through the case study conducted at micro level, it becomes abundantly clear that the initiative and enterprise to consciously develop agriculture still remain concentrated among a small segment of the Indian cultivators and having used different criteria of measurement their proportion roughly comes to about 20 to 25 per cent of the total number of cultivator households. They really have taken cultivation as a business proposition and may be named as the entrepreneurial class in Indian agriculture. Of course, this proportion varies from state to state and most likely will be higher in Group I states than that in Group II sates.

10. The broad findings obtained from the micro-level case

study conducted in two districts of West Bengal do not contradict the main findings derived from our macro-level analysis of the country-wide situation on the basis of secondary data available from official and other sources even though among the cultivator households brought under the coverage of the case study, a large majority are relatively poor households in the sense that they are generally marginal and small holders. But a feature, which emerges out of the case study and which we consider to be specially mentioned here is that a large section of the cultivator households covered in the case study have reported to have set apart a portion of their household earnings as savings and instead of ploughing back the whole amount of the major part of that for development of their own agriculture, they have preferred to invest a major portion of that savings in banks as deposit. Perhaps they consider the return from banks in the form of interest an assured amount compared to the uncertain future return from household agriculture and to meet the cash need for development of their own agriculture, they depend on whatever credit money they can obtain the repayment of which, given the condition prevailing, may be postponed *ad-infinitum*.

Recommendations

1. Since only a small segment of the cultivator households, the proportion of which obviously being not uniform in all states, could transform their farms into a commodity producing business enterprise and the remaining large chunk continued to operate in more or less a subsistence sector with little surplus generation here and there. The main thrust of the programme for revamping agriculture for accelerated development must, therefore, be concentrated on the farm sector. Also since the latter sector remains handicapped in so far as the size of farm-holding, the nature of the capital

structure in farm, the making use of institutional credit facilities, the optimum utilisation of irrigation potential created etc., are concerned, all these factors have to be taken into careful consideration in bringing about improvement and overall change in this sector and it will be an uphill task. In this connection, the pressure of population, particularly in the latter sector, have to be kept in view as introduction of any labour substituting technique may ultimately turn out to be counter productive.

2. Since small size of farm-holding is one of the important factor that decelerate agricultural production and the greatest hindrance standing in the way in bringing about change in technology in farm production and in capital structure of the farm, reform measures to enlarge the size of farm-holding have to be initiated on a high priority basis. Only distribution of vested land to landless will not serve any purpose unless that is combined with effective measures to supply agricultural inputs, water and credit facilities to them. The distribution of vested land to landless will only increase the number of marginal and small holds, the average size of farm-holdings will not thereby increase. So measure to consolidate the holdings, without however impairing the right and ownership of land, have to be taken and implemented.
3. Till now full utilisation of irrigation potential has not been materialised. For a real break through from traditional to moderate technology, water is an essential requirement. Necessary infrastructure to carry the water to the farms, particularly those belonging to the less developed sector mentioned above has to be built up and water rates should be so fixed as the concerned cultivators can bear the load of the water rate. In this connection indiscriminate pumping out of underground water has to be avoided as the situation regarding ground water level is reported to be not very much favourable. All the above is necessary but, diversion of substantial portion from agriculture is essential.

4. Abundant supply of surplus rural manpower dependent on agriculture is another big hindrance which holds back cultivators to venture labour saving or labour substituting technology or to change the capital structure in their farm business. This is particularly very much relevant to the small holding and relatively backward or predominantly traditional farm. Some measures have to be taken to reduce the pressure of population on agriculture. Perhaps a governmental initiative has to be undertaken to encourage setting up of small manufacturing units, mostly agro-based or forest-based where the surplus manpower can be diverted. As our case study has shown, in both the West Bengal districts, because of the manufacturing, trading and service units operating in the districts, the condition of average cultivator households is better than the average households in the state. But only setting up of the units will not help unless effective measures are taken to market the products and also to make available the required raw materials which the individual units can purchase at reasonable market rate.
5. All sections of the cultivators cannot avail the opportunity to utilise the benefit of the expanded credit facilities provided for by the government through the RBI and Commercial Banks. Particularly, the small-holding and poor cultivators are being deprived of these facilities as most of them are considered not credit-worthy and thereby they cannot, even if they desire, bring about even small changes in regard to technology or capital structure in their farm-business. These section of cultivators ultimately fallback upon the non-institutional financial agencies and are forced to pay exorbitant interest. Both the RBI and Commercial Bank must consider why the credit-deposit ratios fixed by different banks cannot be increased so that, another layer of the needy cultivators can avail of the credit-facilities provided for by the government. If the

co-operative banks and other rural banks can afford to increase the ratio at a much high level, why the commercial banks cannot behave in a similar fashion. Of course, the question of repayment has to be always taken care of as the government cannot allow the public fund to drain out. This last point makes a shift of depressed group away from agriculture is essential for a lasting shift to a better economic position in agriculture.

Index